TOMORROW THE WORLD

This is the true account of the experiences of a German girl, Ilse, during the Nazi regime. She was eleven years old when Hitler came to power, and she grew to womanhood against a background of youthful heroics that led to terror, war and ultimately total ruin.

Subsequently she married a British soldier and wrote these memoirs herself, in English.

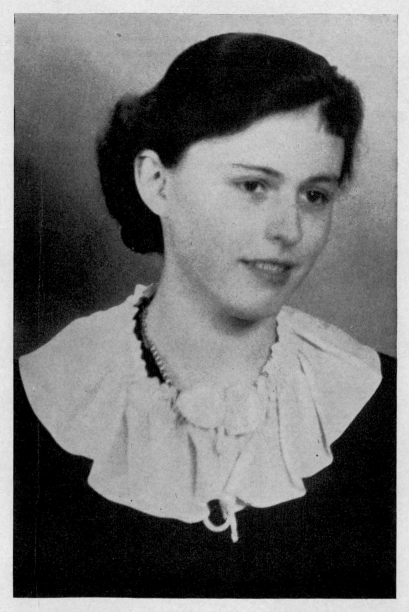

The author, aged fourteen, during her schooldays; she had just started to learn English.

TOMORROW THE WORLD

by

ILSE McKEE

*Illustrated with
eight pages of photographs*

'*Today Germany is ours; and
tomorrow the world*'
(Line from a Hitler Youth song)

LONDON
J. M. DENT & SONS LTD

CONTENTS

ILLUSTRATIONS

' *SIEG, HEIL!* '

In the early 1930's the Nazi Party (National Sozialistische Deutsche Arbeiter Partei, abbreviated as N.S.D.A.P.) became the largest political party in Germany. Its essential nature was not so much that of an ordinary political movement as of a private army. Hitler had gained more votes than anyone else, but he was never able to achieve an absolute majority over all the other parties combined; he came to power in January 1933, and the intrigue by which he arrived was incidental to this fact, that his party was not a collection of voters but a mass movement capable of using organized force. Hitler was nevertheless very careful to conform to the outward trappings of legality.

Once he had achieved power, he set out to extend his authority to every corner of the state so that government should be the unbridled will of one man instead of, as it normally is, a balance between various forces and interests in the state. To suppress the traditional sources of power he needed mass support; and he got it by acting decisively to satisfy the patriotic and socialistic leanings of the common man. Within a few years he produced a 'Greater Germany' which, like Cromwell's Commonwealth, was the terror of her foes abroad.

I WAS born on a bitterly cold day in January 1922, the second daughter in an upper-middle-class family of academic background.

All my relatives held some academic degree or other and were well established in their professions. My ancestors included architects, musicians (amongst them Johann Strauss, the Waltz King), teachers and, on my mother's side, titled officers who had served the dukes of Saxony. My father taught English,

French and German at a local grammar school for boys. His salary was excellent and more than sufficient to keep his little family in comfort.

Our town of sixty thousand inhabitants contained a lovely theatre built by the Duke of Saxony, who used to live in the old castle on top of the Porphyrrock. However, the dukes were all gone now, and the castle was used for special festivals and as a museum. Dramatic performances were held in the grounds in the open air.

My father was a deeply religious man of very sensitive and artistic temperament. He loved music and played the piano beautifully. His sense of honour and duty, like that of most decent people in Germany, was absolutely rigid. My mother was tiny and fragile, with golden hair and violet-blue eyes. She was partly Austrian. Sweet-tempered, sensible and well balanced, she was just the right partner for my highly emotional father. Her intelligence was far above average and she spoke English and French fluently, making poor Father rather jealous, for though he was an excellent teacher he could never quite equal her in quickness of mind and expression. In appearance he was her direct opposite, very dark, with blue-black hair and black eyes. He looked a bit like a Hungarian gipsy. In fact it was said that the family had some Hungarian blood in them. There were others amongst his ancestors who had lived in southern France, but they had left their country during the Huguenot troubles and settled in Germany.

My sister Erica was nearly eight years old when I was born. She was a difficult, highly strung child, and she was very jealous at first, though later on I think she came to love me in her own selfish and moody way.

Here I was then, born into a Germany of political unrest, faction, uncertainty, combined with poverty, unemployment and the hurt pride that resulted from the humiliating terms of the Versailles Treaty at the end of the First World War. I grew into a dreamy, plump little thing and everybody said that I promised to be a great beauty one day. I was of course completely oblivious of anything going on around me, except for the things that affected my own family. After all, what was there to worry about? I did not know hardship of any kind; I never went to bed hungry or out on a cold day in inadequate clothes; my father was not unemployed nor ever likely to be. Until I started school I thus grew up in the belief that the world was a very happy place indeed.

It was during my second year in a government primary school that I realized for the first time the existence of a world outside my own happy life, full of trouble, danger and unpleasantness. On my way home from school one afternoon I got mixed up in a demonstration procession of the Communist Party. Men were carrying red banners, a band was playing, women were shouting and gesticulating. I was shocked to recognize amongst them the fathers or mothers of some of my schoolmates. They carried boards with slogans, such as 'Proletarians of All Nations Unite' or 'Vote for Ernst Thälmann.' From time to time some of them would raise their clenched fists in a salute to the onlookers, and the next moment they would all burst into a shouting chorus of the Internationale, the battle-song of the German Communist Party.

Their shabbiness and determination seemed to me infinitely menacing; and yet, like any other seven-year-old, I stood in fascination and watched. A lot of people started to walk away quickly but the procession moved on, shouting and singing in a most provocative manner. Suddenly somebody touched my arm, and I turned round to find myself looking into the anxious eyes of an old lady.

'Run home, child, this is no place for a little girl,' she said. 'For God's sake run home quickly. They might start shooting any moment.'

For an instant I stared at her in utter amazement, unable to grasp the meaning of her words, but the urgency and fright in her voice were enough to make me realize that I was in danger, and without a word to her I fled.

I soon forgot the incident, and all I can recall of the following two years is that people talked a lot about Field Marshal von Hindenburg and somebody called Adolf Hitler. Every time those two names were mentioned in a conversation I knew I should be bored by the talk that followed. Politics were not in my line.

Five days after my eleventh birthday—on 30th January 1933—Adolf Hitler became Reichschancellor of Germany. It was a day to be remembered by everyone. The whole country seemed to be in an uproar of excitement and expectation. Radios were bawling away in all the public squares, giving the news and announcing the plans the new chancellor had for the future of Germany.

My father was very quiet when he came home from work that day. In answer to my countless questions he told me that Adolf Hitler had been the leader of the National Socialist Party. This party had not been very large to begin with, but it had grown considerably in strength and power. Still Father could not understand how Hitler had managed to come right to the top. However, the man's intentions seemed good and one could only hope that he would be the right person to lead Germany.

There were five million unemployed men in the country at the time. That meant that, with the families of those men, roughly twenty-five million Germans were living in poverty. The problem was big enough to make any nation look desperately for a strong man who would do more than merely talk. Germany was ripe for Hitler.

My constant playmate, a little girl called Gabriela, came from the poorer classes. Her father was a night porter in a factory and a confirmed Communist; the mother was half gipsy and a devout Methodist. Gabriela herself was of almost angelic beauty, with golden hair and deep blue eyes.

She was unhappy at home. Our house offered a kind of asylum for her where she could hide from her father's tantrums. He used to beat mother and child in the most cruel manner, so she simply stayed away from home as much as she could. She often stole little things from our house, but I was determined to ignore that as I loved her dearly.

Our friendship lasted until I started at the grammar school. After that she avoided me, for with that step the division of the social classes begins. Only twice more did she seek my love and sympathy. The first time was when her father had hanged himself, partly for political reasons because Hitler had come to power, and partly because he was suffering from syphilis in the final stages.

The second time was when at eighteen she was expecting a baby by her uncle, a married man many years her senior. He had no intention whatever of marrying her. She had stayed for a short holiday with the family, and, sensing her readiness, the man had seduced her under the eyes of his own wife and family. As he was fairly high up in the ranks of the N.S.D.A.P., the matter was hushed up to avoid a scandal. He gave her a generous allowance to pay for the child's upbringing and education, and apart from having made a fool of herself she was none the worse for it. She partly blamed herself for what had happened. I went to see her shortly after the baby was born and she quite frankly admitted it.

'I had to do it,' she said. 'You probably won't understand. You have lived a sheltered life, and your parents have provided you with everything you want. You have never seen your father beat your mother until she was half dead, or try even to assault his own daughter. I have; and I have known hunger, and many other unpleasant things. This was a change, something new and exciting. I just could not help myself.'

B

I was shocked, but we parted in quite a friendly manner, though we did not seek each other's company again.

School for all German children starts at the age of six. The primary schools are run by the Government and are free. Everybody has to attend for four years. Then parents who have the means can send their children to a grammar school, where at high fees education is continued for another nine years before the final examination which qualifies a student to go on to the university and study for a degree.

My four years at the primary school revealed an entirely new order of life to me. Children from all the social classes attended. Many had lice and were sent for treatment before they were allowed to continue at school. One of my classmates disclosed to me the facts of life. She came from a poor family, the mother and father and about seven brothers and sisters all living and sleeping in one room. The father was a drunken brute. The girl was extremely proud of the knowledge of sexual matters she had thus acquired at home, and conveyed it to me triumphantly, but with the help of my loving and wise parents I managed to take this hurdle safely.

Once I had a terrible fight with one of my classmates about the religious lessons. In those days parents who were atheists were not obliged to let their children take part in religious instruction. Thus as soon as our lesson was due this girl would slip away quietly and go home. It seemed incredible to me that there should be people in this world who did not believe in God and our Lord Jesus Christ, so one day I beat her up. The poor child's nose was bleeding by the time our lady teacher arrived and stopped me. When the lesson was over she called me to the desk, and after the other children had left the class-room she explained to me gently and kindly and made me see my terrible error. Soon afterwards, to my great relief, the child joined us in our religious instruction and seemed happier for it. Obviously our teacher had spoken to the parents, who had dealt with the problem intelligently.

In spring 1932 I passed an examination and changed over to the only local grammar school for girls. The atmosphere at the new school was different. All the girls had the same social background and the relationship between teacher and pupil was far more personal. At the government school I had just been one of many; at my new school I was treated as an individual, and I throve on it.

After Hitler became chancellor things began to change in Germany. Great provisions were being made for the working classes to ease their lot and improve their standard of living. New houses were being built everywhere and the old slums torn down. There was going to be work for everyone. Fewer and fewer unemployed men were hanging round the cigarette and beer kiosks down by the cinema, shouting, arguing and drinking. People were wearing better clothes and could afford to buy sufficient food for their families.

Slowly the bait worked. Even those who had been rigidly against Hitler before now became ardent followers. The various youth clubs were closed down and the Hitler Youth Organization took their place. Freemasonry was strictly forbidden. Old Comrades and student organizations were taken over by the Party. There was hardly anything which was not N.S.

Then came the Röhm affair and with it countless arrests of members of well-known families in the town, including boys of the Hitler Youth and schoolboys. Röhm, it was said, had been the leader of a secret organization of homosexuals, and homosexuality had spread all over Germany, even as far as the Hitler Youth. The Government was determined to stamp this sort of thing out completely.

A number of boys I used to know were arrested during lessons at school. Some of them we never saw again. A whole circle of families who had practised perversion at secret meetings in their homes were taken, both men and women. Some of them were reprieved and later on forced to marry and raise a family.

Adolf Hitler did them a good turn by forcing them to go back to leading a normal life. As far as I know there were no relapses.

As the years went by the pressure on everyone who had not joined the Party increased steadily. Those who did not join felt they were outcasts. At last, with a heavy heart and many doubts, Father let me join the Hitler Youth, and he became a member of the N.S.D.A.P. himself. The fact that his nerves were bad and that he suffered from severe attacks of asthma protected him from any active service.

Things were quite different for me though. I, and all the other girls of my age, had to attend evening classes twice weekly. We had to be present at every public meeting and at youth rallies and sports. The week-ends were crammed full with outings, campings and marches when we carried heavy packs on our backs. It was all fun in a way and we certainly got plenty of exercise, but it had a bad effect on our school reports. There was hardly ever any time now for homework.

The evening classes were conducted by young girls, usually hardly older than we were ourselves. These young B.D.M.[1] leaders taught us songs and tried desperately to maintain a certain amount of discipline without ever really succeeding. In summer, instead of conducting the class, they would give us a few hours' drill in the yard. We were marched up and down as if we were soldiers on the barrack square, with a girl leader barking orders at us like a regimental sergeant-major.

We were of course lectured a lot on National Socialist ideology, and most of this went right over our heads. In most cases the young girl leader did not know herself what she was talking about. We were told from a very early age to prepare for motherhood, as the mother in the eyes of our beloved leader and the National Socialist Government was the most important person in the nation. We were Germany's hope in the future, and it was our duty to breed and rear the new generation of

---

[1] Bund Deutsche Mädel (German Girls' Organization), the equivalent for girls of the Hitler Youth (membership compulsory).

sons and daughters who would carry on the tradition of the thousand-year-old Reich.

The boys' evening classes were run in exactly the same way and in the same building. Frequently we would all have to go to the auditorium, where some important personage would give a lecture on racial problems and the necessity of raising the birth-rate. He too would remind us of our duties as future fathers and mothers of the nation, and somehow I never managed to suppress a giggle when I looked at those spidery-legged, pimply little cockerels who were supposed to become the fathers of our children.

These lessons soon bore fruit in the shape of quite a few illegitimate small sons and daughters for the Reich, brought forth by teenage members of the B.D.M. and conceived in the grounds of our Hitler Youth Home. The girls felt that they had done their duty and seemed remarkably unconcerned about the scandal. The possible fathers could be heard proudly debating as to who had done it, whenever there was a chance that the girls might be able to overhear.

I soon got tired of it all and frequently found some reason for excusing myself from the evening classes. My education took up more and more of my time now, and doing my homework was a far more satisfying occupation to my inquisitive mind. It also brought my school report up again to a decent level. That this attitude earned me the reputation of a shirker did not worry me much, as there were quite a number of other girls who did exactly the same.

Then came the 'Crystal Night,' a pogrom against the Jewish race. We did not hear or see much, as our house was on the outskirts of the town, but we saw the glow of the synagogue as it was burned down. The next morning the town was full of rumours and I soon found out what had happened from those girls in our class whose fathers had taken part. I felt shocked and surprised, but they were proud and happy, convinced that justice had been done.

My father's reaction was one of sad bewilderment: 'Fancy taking old Levy,' he said over and over again. 'He won the Iron Cross First Class while fighting for Germany during the Great War. It was in his store and through his connections that our starving children were fed by the Quaker organization in 1917-18. Have they no shame to take such a man and humiliate him?'

The windows of Mr Levy's large store had been smashed and now the store was closed down. His twin daughters, Lotte and Lore, had not come to school that morning. We knew they were still in the town, but it was obvious that they would leave as soon as possible to avoid further aggressions. The family had been liked and respected and I am sure that most of us had misgivings about this rash and mean action on the part of the new Government.

The twin girls were in my class. Lotte was a pert, confident girl of outstanding intelligence. She was also full of fun and wit. Lore was shy and very quiet, a serious, dreamy girl of fascinating beauty. Her delicately shaped face was framed by a mop of blue-black curls. Her nose was straight, and her pale skin contrasted most effectively with the vivid deep blue of her eyes. It was partly the dreamy, absent-minded expression in her eyes that made her so incredibly attractive and lovable. I kept my fingers crossed for her in particular, hoping she would not come to any harm. She seemed so defenceless and sweet.

Years later I was told that, with her father and mother, she died miserably in a concentration camp. The rest of the family, Lotte and two brothers, got away safely. Mr Levy had invested most of his fortune abroad, and the three surviving children used it to build up a new business in Cairo.

One morning at school we were all led to the auditorium to hear an announcement from one of the senior teachers. What he had to say came as a terrible shock to all of us. Our headmaster, whom we had loved and admired, had been found dead in his flat the previous evening. He had hanged himself.

A widower for many years, he had befriended an unmarried Jewish lady teacher and had gradually grown very fond of her. Owing to her undesirable racial status she had been dismissed from her job, and was now earning a small living by private tutoring for which the Government had been generous enough to give a concession. Several times the girl had urged our headmaster to break off the association, warning him that sooner or later their friendship would have repercussions for him. He refused to listen. He was lonely and needed her affection and understanding. Without her life would have been quite meaningless.

The inevitable happened. Someone dropped a hint in the right quarters about the affair. Before they could get him, however, he had made his decision. He preferred death to humiliation. He made a will before he died and left all his worldly possessions, a very substantial gift, to his lady friend. The Government could do nothing to stop the legal proceedings.

As a last sign of our gratitude and love we gave our old headmaster one of the most magnificent funerals our town had ever seen. It was like a protest against intrusion and terror. I can hardly think of anyone who did not take part in order to pay him their last respects.

Six months later our music teacher died in the same tragic way. He was a very religious man and inclined to be melancholy. The campaign against the Church had started, and I think he found that he could not come to terms both with himself and the new Government regarding it. In an attack of deepest depression he must have made his mind up to end his life.

Yet these events could not really damp our enthusiasm. Hitler had put Germany back on her feet. Everything seemed to have changed for the better and our faith in him grew stronger and stronger with each of his new achievements.

During my third year at the grammar school a great change in the whole educational system took place. The nine years required to obtain the school certificate were reduced to eight. Every subject was now presented from the National Socialist point of view. Most of the old lecture books were replaced by new ones which had been written, compiled and censored by government officials. Adolf Hitler's *Mein Kampf* became the textbook for our history lessons. We read and discussed it with our master, chapter by chapter, and when we had finished we started again from the beginning. Even though we were supposed to know the contents of the book almost by heart nothing much ever stuck in my mind. I hated politics and distrusted politicians, but I thought, as most people did, that Hitler was far above intrigue and perfidy and would prove to be the saviour that Germany needed. Even so I found his book dull and boring. Rosenberg's *Myth of the Twentieth Century*, which the majority of thinking Germans regarded as a bad joke, was the next most important book to *Mein Kampf*. A new subject, the science of the races, was introduced, and religious instruction became optional.

Our school had always been run on very conservative lines and I am sure the situation was difficult for our teachers. Most of them had been doubtful about Hitler, but unless they wanted to lose their jobs they had to make a violent turn in his direction. Even if they sympathized with my attitude towards politics, they could not afford to let me get away with it. Some of the children in each class would not hesitate to act as informers. The Government was probing into the past history of every teacher, exploring his political background. Many were dismissed and it was dangerous to act as anything but a National Socialist.

Once I attended one of the big youth rallies. It was held at Weimar. As I should have to stay away from home for two or three days my father was reluctant to let me go. I was only thirteen, too young in his opinion to go anywhere without the protection of at least one parent, and he had not much faith in our young girl leaders who were to look after us. I promised that I would be very careful in every respect, and he finally gave in.

We were taken to Weimar by coach. Rooms had been booked for us beforehand in private households. I was accommodated by a very nice elderly couple, who seemed delighted to have me and treated me like a daughter. Early the next morning the coach picked me up at my billet to take me, along with all the other girls, to the stadium.

This was such an immense place that most of it was out of our range of view and we could see what was happening only in our own section. Many bands made their ceremonial entry into the great arena and marched round, each one with its own special military appeal. But the one I shall never forget consisted of about twenty-four young boys whose performance was so awe-inspiring that every time they marched past there was a hush. This band was called 'The Drums.'

The actual drums were very long, reaching from the waist to the knee, and they made an uncanny sound, hollow and threatening, as the boys beat them to the rhythm of the quick march. There was something symbolic about them. The monotony of the low-pitched beat, following the same pattern of rhythm over and over again, made me involuntarily think of doom.

These drum bands were meant to remind us of the drummer boys of hundreds of years ago, who had marched into battle ignoring the wounds they received, drumming until they fell and died. Their unlimited courage was meant to be an example for us throughout our lives. A poem I had learned at school came back into my mind:

> In Germany there sounds a drum,
> And he who beats it leads.
> Those who follow, follow dumb:
> They are his chosen flock.
>
> Upon the flag they swear their oath,
> Blood brotherhood, and faith.
> He beats their fate, the path they tread,
> His face an iron mask.

The leader marches towards the sun
With utmost power and strength;
And you, O people, are his drum,
Awakening to your fate.[1]

While the bands played, the gymnasts marched in. The boys, who were dressed in black P.T. kit, formed themselves into the shape of a giant swastika on the arena floor; then the girls, in white P.T. kit, formed a circle around the swastika of boys. Next the gymnasts started to perform, accompanied by appropriate music blaring from the various loudspeakers, and all the while they kept their formation as a gigantic black swastika in a white circle.

Races followed later and, during a sixty-minute break, girls in white dancing dresses performed folk-dances round the maypoles. Then there were more races, followed by a P.T. demonstration given by the younger age group of which I was a member. For this we wore black shorts and white sleeveless vests, and were rather cold. When it came to the prize-giving we were too far away to see anything and too worn out to bother to listen to the results which were announced over the loudspeakers.

To conclude, the boys and girls once more formed the swastika. The area Hitler Youth leader gave a speech and when he had finished we stood at attention at the salute and sang the Hitler Youth song.

[1] Here is the German version of the poem:

Eine Trommel geht in Deutschland um,
Und der sie schlägt der führt,
Und die ihm folgen, folgen stumm,
Sie sind von ihm gekuert.

Sie schwören ihm den Fahneneid,
Gefolgschaft und Gericht,
Er trommelt ihres Schicksals Spur,
Mit ehernem Gesicht.

Der Führer geht der Sonne zu,
Mit angespannter Kraft,
Und seine Trommel, die bist du,
Volk, werde Leidenschaft!

Finally the leader stepped forward and shouted: 'Adolf Hitler.' We replied: 'Sieg, Heil! Sieg, Heil! Sieg, Heil!' We yelled these words with all the strength our lungs could muster, and they sounded enormously powerful.

One day we got a new classmate. She was the daughter of an opera singer from Berlin who had been engaged as the tenor at the local theatre. Her name was Tony and she was a clever, pert and lively girl. Though she was nothing much to look at, her acting talent made up completely for her lack of beauty. She was a wonderful comedienne. Between lectures, during the ten-minute breaks, she used to recite poems for us, romantic and dramatic ones, written by our great classic poets, and she made a parody of them. We laughed so much that we invariably ended up under our tables, begging her to stop. So far we had always managed to pull ourselves together before our master came in for the next lesson, but one day Tony left it too late.

She was reciting Schiller's 'Die Glocke,' the story of a bell being cast. She started off by calling her imaginary apprentices together with much shouting and cheerful throaty laughter. As soon as these irresponsible hoodlums had turned up, she told them to get the mould prepared. Then she asked for blessings from heaven, imploring the Lord to help her to complete the difficult task successfully, and with much gesturing, rolling of eyeballs and noticeable backache she proceeded to mix the metals for the final cast.

Outside the bell rang for the new lesson to begin. We were all shrieking with laughter, but some of us made a feeble though vain attempt to draw her attention to it. The huge fire which was necessary to melt the metals was apparently unbearably hot, for she started to strip. After she had taken off her cardigan and wiped her sweating brow she stirred the liquid mixture of the metals viciously, for by now they had all melted and everything was ready for the cast. She was just cupping her hands to her mouth, shouting angrily for her careless apprentices, who as usual had disappeared at the vital moment, when our master came in.

There was an instant of shuffle, some suppressed giggles, and we were all on our feet as if nothing had happened. For a moment Dr Fahl looked at us, then he watched Tony slipping quietly back into her seat, and with a puzzled frown he sat down on his chair by the desk.

'Well, girls,' announced Dr Fahl after a few moments of shaky silence, 'it's poetry today, and the subject is Schiller's "Glocke," isn't it? We discussed it in our last poetry lesson, and I told you to learn the first quarter of it by heart.'

Giggles were leaping up like little flames. For a moment Dr Fahl looked up from the book which he now had in front of him.

'Right, now,' he continued, 'I have my notebook here and you'll get marks for your performance. I hope you have learned hard at home, and will all do very well today.'

He picked up his pencil and looked round the class scrutinizing us. 'Tony,' he called, making up his mind at last and craning his neck in her direction, 'will you come forward, please, and begin.'

The moment Tony opened her mouth for the recital the whole class burst into an explosion of laughter. Dr Fahl's head came up with a jerk at the unfamiliar sound.

'Tony,' he demanded, 'what is all this about? Explain at once. Or don't you know?'

Tony stood wringing her hands, while the rest of us were lolling about in uncontrollable laughter. 'No,' she squeaked, shaking her head in a desperate effort to stay serious, 'I don't, sir, honestly I don't.'

Tony's wit and intelligence were far superior to ours, and she beat us in all subjects. We admired her immensely and soon a little circle of girls was forming to be her closest friends. I was amongst them. But several girls in our class who were quite high up in the ranks of the Hitler Youth, even though they were in awe of her intelligence and ever so slightly jealous, kept strictly away from her and did not hesitate from time to time to make slanderous remarks about her family.

Tony's mother was a charming woman, a Jewess, though I did not know that at the time. I often went to visit them in their little flat, and if Tony was out her mother would invite me to stay for a chat. I think she was fond of me, for otherwise she would not have talked so freely about her private affairs. She was worried about the relationship between Tony and her father. Like many highly artistic people, the girl was wild and unmanageable. Her resentment at parental authority took the form of provocative resistance. This attitude used to drive the father into murderous rages. He would beat Tony terribly and if the mother tried to interfere he would beat her as well.

One summer evening I went to visit them as usual and found the mother alone in the flat. Tony and her father had gone to the theatre to look at some new costumes. They were Hungarian folk dresses and Tony hoped to borrow one for a forthcoming fancy-dress party. After she had let me into the flat Mrs Schwartz went back to her chair on the rostrum by the window, where she used to do her needlework. Darkness was beginning to fall. It was very quiet in the room and very stuffy.

Mrs Schwartz seemed unusually sad that day, and as I watched her profile outlined against the window a feeling of sorrow and tragedy crept unaccountably over me. She looked beaten and resigned. She had put down her mending and her hands lay quietly in her lap, resting on the sock she had just been darning. She seemed preoccupied and silent and her thoughts were clearly wandering. We sat there in the semi-darkness and neither of us spoke for a long time.

'Well, child,' said Frau Schwartz at last, 'Germany has come up in the world, hasn't she? Hitler has achieved a lot during the last few years.'

That was a strange opening, and I felt a little surprised. She had never discussed politics with me before.

'If he means to carry on like that,' she continued, 'I should say that you all have a wonderful future ahead of you.'

I nodded approval, wondering secretly what the real reason for this strange conversation could be.

'It's not so good for us, though,' she said.

'Why?' I asked.

She looked round at me in complete surprise. 'Why, child, don't you know? I'm a Jewess.' She gave me a sweet indulgent smile. 'Well, well, you are a little innocent, aren't you? You have instruction about the races at school, haven't you? I should have thought you would have noticed.'

I stared at her, completely taken aback, noting down in my mind all the details in her face which we had been taught were supposed to be typical of her race. They were all there and I had never noticed them.

'No,' I said at last. 'I didn't know. I am sorry.' I could have bitten my tongue the moment the last remark had slipped out. What a silly, tactless thing to say under the circumstances!

She smiled. 'You needn't be sorry,' she said quietly. 'It's quite all right with me. The one I'm really worried about is Tony. They'll get me first, and then they will come for her. She is half Jew after all, and they won't be prepared to overlook that.'

'Are you talking about the Gestapo, Frau Schwartz?' I asked.

'Yes, the Gestapo.'

'Does anyone know you are a Jewess?'

She gave an amused little chuckle. 'Oh, of course. They aren't all as innocent as you are, my dear. Only a little while ago my husband got a warning. A "good friend" advised him to get a divorce and get rid of me as quickly as possible unless he wanted to lose his job.'

'Very nice of him, I must say, but are you quite sure it's not just the usual gossip of some interfering characters? Why on earth should anyone want to harm you or Tony? You've never done a wrong thing in all your life. The whole thing seems preposterous.'

She shook her head. 'God bless you, child, for your wonderful optimism. But I'm afraid it won't work. The Gestapo are on my trail, I'm sure. It's serious, and I think it would be best for me to clear out before they actually turn up here.'

'Oh, but you mustn't do that,' I cried. 'Your husband and Tony will be completely lost without you. They'll kill each other with their terrible tempers.'

'If I don't go, dear child, I shall be taken. In either case those two will have to get used to living without me. They'll soon learn. As long as they don't touch Tony I shall be quite happy.'

I looked up at the quiet woman sitting on the rostrum. My mind took in every detail of her kind, sad face and my heart ached for her at the thought of the tragedy which had suddenly befallen the whole family. I felt angry and frustrated that there was nothing I could do to stop this madness, nothing anybody could do to prevent grief and misery. Things would take their course.

A few days later Frau Schwartz was gone. She had disappeared quietly, leaving a letter of farewell for her husband and Tony. In it she urged them to stand by each other firmly. Together they would be able to face whatever lay ahead of them, and on no account did she want them to try to trace her.

Tony was inconsolable. She had loved her mother deeply. For a long time all her old zest seemed to have gone out of her. She was listless and lonely, and often she just sat and cried.

Years later I met Tony again in Munich. It was a strange coincidence, a chance in a million. We ran into each other at the Odeonsplatz. I had visited the city to spend a few days there with my fiancé, and one morning, strolling out alone, I saw her. I recognized her at once, but she brushed past me, pretending not to know me. I followed her. She was quite angry when I addressed her.

'For God's sake, Tony,' I said, getting hold of her arm, 'what's the matter? Surely you remember me, your former classmate in A?'

'No,' she said rudely, 'I don't think I do, and anyway I should hardly consider myself to be the right company for anyone.'

'Oh, come now,' I said, a little exasperated, 'don't be so silly. Let's go and have a cup of coffee somewhere, for old times' sake.'

She turned her head and smiled at me, giving in to my gentle coaxing.

'Oh, all right,' she said, 'if you insist. I know just the place where we can sit and talk in peace and quiet. Even the coffee isn't too bad.'

I slipped my arm through hers. 'That's much better, Tony,' I said. 'How lucky John couldn't get away from the aerodrome this morning. But for him we would never have met today.'

'John?' she asked. 'Who's John? Are you married, Ilse?'

'No, not yet, but don't let's talk about me. Tell me what you have done with yourself all these years.'

Over a cup of hot coffee she told me her story. It wasn't a very happy one. Her mother was dead. She had died in a concentration camp. A short note from the authorities had informed her and her father about that fact. Just a few cold words, with no explanation as to how she had died. The death certificate had been enclosed in the letter. Her father had retired and lived on a very small pension. He rented a room somewhere in Munich, but she did not know where. They had parted a long time ago. His pension was far too small for two people to live on.

For a living Tony did some part-time work as a typist. The

money she earned was not enough to live on. She had had some lessons in drama and acting, but no good-class theatre would employ half-Jewish actresses nowadays. She had to give that up. Sometimes, when the money got really short, she prostituted herself.

'I have come down in the world, haven't I?' she said.

I offered her a cigarette and she took it gratefully.

'Oh, forget it. You are you,' I said. 'This sort of thing can't last for ever. Soon your luck will turn, and then you will think all this has just been a bad dream.'

I offered her my matches and there was a dreamy expression on her face as she lit her cigarette. She inhaled deeply, enjoying herself, and then she smiled at me through a screen of smoke.

'Oh, Ilse,' she said dreamily, 'do you remember the fun we had at school? Remember that day when I recited "Die Glocke" and Dr Fahl caught us in the act? God, how you all laughed! It's like a dream now, the sort of dream I should like to dream again, straight away, until this nightmare life is over.'

Suddenly she asked me a strange question. 'Do you think your fiancé could find me a little job at the aerodrome, Ilse?'

'How?'

'Oh, it was just an idea. Forget it. Of course he can't. He's got his career to think of. They wouldn't like him to bring along a half-Jew clerk or typist. I must be mad. I get the most crazy ideas lately. I suppose it's just that one is inclined to cling to the last straw of hope.'

She gathered up her bag and gloves and, getting up from her chair, held out her hand.

'Goodbye, Ilse,' she said. 'It's done me good to have met you again. I'll feel a lot better now for a little while. You know, Mother thought the world of you. Well, so long. The best of luck and I hope you will be very happy. You certainly deserve it.'

c

She walked out of the café quickly, giving me a sad little salute with her right hand just before she slipped through the door.   Before I even made an attempt to follow her the crowd of pedestrians in the street outside had swallowed her up and she was gone.

2

I SEE THE FÜHRER

Hitler's early conquests, obtained virtually without bloodshed
and with relatively little foreign reaction, were not of a sort likely
to antagonize the Germans; he reiterated constantly that he had
been a front-line soldier himself and would never consent to
another bloodbath. But in 1936 came the first rumblings of
world war when a revolt in Spain led to a civil conflict in which
part of the armed forces of Germany, Italy and Russia were also
engaged. From then on events moved rapidly. The interven-
tion of the Russians was taken by Hitler as an excuse to sign an
Anti-Comintern Pact with Japan in November 1936; he took
advantage of the imminent victory of Franco by annexing Austria
in March 1938, and shortly afterwards sparked off a crisis by
demanding that the Czech Sudetenland should be handed over to
him. This crisis was resolved by the Munich Agreement which
gave Hitler what he wanted. So far he had been annexing only
German-speaking peoples; had he left it at that he might have
survived. But in November 1938 there was a violent anti-Jewish
pogrom in Germany, sparked off by the murder by a Jew of a
German diplomat in Paris, followed in March 1939 by the sub-
jugation of all Czechoslovakia, and in the summer of 1939 by
demands upon the Polish Government for the cession of Danzig.
Dazzled by success, Hitler was out to get all he could while the
going was good. On 1st September 1939 German troops crossed
the Polish border.

ONE OF my closer friends at school was a girl called
Belle. She came from an old aristocratic family and
her father owned property and land out in the country.
He was the perfect example of the old country squire, authorita-
tive, jovial and very proud of his blue blood. He was over six
feet tall and very heavily built.

The family lived in a large mansion in the country, about six kilometres from my home town. Their means of transport consisted of two lovely open coaches drawn by black ponies. They were a large family, if all the aunts, nephews and nieces were included, but the size of the mansion guaranteed sufficient privacy for all of them. They hardly ever saw one another except at meals, which they all took together in the large oak-panelled dining-room.

The old squire's wife was a beautiful golden-haired woman in her late thirties, a baroness by birth and a true lady in character and manner. Belle was their eldest daughter, and she had two sisters. Unfortunately there were no boys. Belle was almost as tall as her father but slim and perfectly proportioned. Her gleaming copper-coloured hair reached right down to her knees.

For some time I used to spend almost every week-end with them at their beautiful house. Belle liked my company and invited me frequently. I loved those week-ends. I enjoyed the ride in the open carriage drawn by those lovely ponies. The care and attention I received from Belle's mother and all the servants flattered my little ego and made me feel like a great lady in disguise.

A chambermaid would take me up to the bathroom and help me freshen up. Then the large gong in the hall would sound for luncheon. There were never less than sixteen people seated round the large oak table in the dining-room. Belle's father would take his seat at the head of the table and we would all bend our heads and fold our hands in our laps while he said grace.

In Germany children and youngsters are not allowed to talk during mealtimes, but that did not stop us from listening attentively to what the grown-ups were saying and discussing it afterwards when we were on our own.

It was at these luncheons at Belle's house that I had an opportunity to find out what the aristocracy in general were thinking of Hitler and his Government, for these were the subjects they discussed most frequently at table.

I was surprised and slightly shocked to hear them refer to Hitler as a parvenu and painter's apprentice, deprecating his lack of background and breeding. They did so openly in front of the servants, and this attitude astounded me. For me it was as if all values had suddenly been reversed. At school and in the Hitler Youth the rise of Hitler from lance-corporal to leader of seventy million people had been presented as a great and undeniable achievement, whereas these people claimed that his humble origins made him unsuitable for such a position. Belle's father predicted a grave future for Germany under Hitler's leadership. In my mind I dismissed this possibility.

As it turned out events proved Belle's father right both for Germany and for himself and his family. Shortly after the war he was shot through the heart by a Polish D.P. in his own farmyard as he was trying to stop the ransacking of his home. When the Russians came his wife and children were turned from their land and obliged to join the innumerable dispossessed refugees.

I was fourteen when I met my first Englishman. He came to Germany through the scheme of exchange visits for school boys and girls. Michael stayed with the family of one of my father's closest friends, the headmaster of the school at which he taught. In exchange, one of his two sons had gone to stay with Michael's parents. As our two families had always visited each other frequently it was only natural now that Michael should be included in our happy gatherings.

He was a Celt if ever there was one. Over six feet tall, with coppery hair, blue eyes and freckles across the bridge of his nose, he seemed to me to be the most handsome and attractive creature I had ever met. He was two years my senior, and as we had both attended evening classes in ballroom dancing we made the most of this advantage. I was enchanted with his delightful manners and the gentle and observant way in which he treated me. A true gentleman already at sixteen, he became my first great infatuation.

The day he left for England all the members of our two families saw him to the train.

'Well,' he said, smiling down at us from the open carriage window and shaking hands all round, 'you have given me a really wonderful time. Thank you very much and I hope I shall see you all in England one day in order to repay your kindness.'

The next year we had another suicide in our school. This time it was my much-loved master in history. He was a wonderful man and his sudden death shook me deeply. He had been a Conservative before Hitler came to power, and from some of the remarks he used to make during lessons we concluded that he was still loyal to the German Emperor Wilhelm. He had been punished for his former activities in the Conservative Party by being demoted from headmaster of a large grammar school in Kassel to an ordinary teacher at our school. There was never any question of a concentration camp in cases like this; it was simply a matter of taking one step down the ladder professionally instead of up.

His daughter was an ardent follower of Hitler. She was in her teens and held a high rank in the Hitler Youth Organization. She was proud of her commission and despised her father for his old-fashioned ideas. This difference in political outlook caused dreadful rows between father and daughter. Distressed and completely helpless, our master had to watch his happy home life crumble to pieces as mutual trust and understanding within the family were replaced by suspicion and dislike. Our master's wife was a quiet, gentle woman who had always been completely disinterested in political issues of any kind. It must have been for her sake that he decided to take his own life, hoping that his death would at least bring peace to her life again.

To the German people's pride and satisfaction, Germany was now regaining her former power and prestige amongst the other European nations. The payment of reparation money to the Western Allies for the 1914–18 war had been called off by Hitler, and our armed forces had been built up and organized better than ever before. Austria had been annexed and the Sudetengau had been handed over to us. Hitler was a great man, a genius, a person sent to us from heaven.

The last summer before I was due to leave school we went on a tour through the Alps and Bavaria. Two other families joined us. They were good friends of ours, and in the end our party consisted of not fewer than twelve people. We were going by road, and as there were so many of us and only three cars to take passengers and luggage, we had to squeeze ourselves into the seats. Rumours of an impending war were spreading steadily but we did not worry unduly. We were convinced that Hitler was a man of peace and would do everything he could to settle things peacefully.

We left early one Monday morning. It was a beautiful clear day and we were all in high spirits. We made a wonderful tour right through Bavaria and Austria, then went on to the Bodensee and finished up with a two-day stay in Munich.

The big city was a spectacle. The streets were lined with masts from which huge flags of black-white-red, or red flags with swastikas, were billowing in the breeze. Red banners with slogans written on them stretched from one side of the street to the other. Each one said something different, 'Munich greets our Führer,' or 'Heil Adolf Hitler,' or 'Long live our Führer,' or 'Germany is Adolf Hitler, and Adolf Hitler is Germany.'

We seemed to have arrived just at the right moment. The

city was chock-a-block with people from all parts of the world. There was a policeman at every corner directing the flood of traffic. Our cars moved at walking pace most of the time, and after a little while we decided to turn into some side road so that we could have a snack and find out what was going on.

We parked the cars outside a little pub and got out. The place was packed with customers. We went over to the counter and ordered some coffee and sandwiches. There was no room to sit down. The proprietor told us that we had arrived in the middle of the preparations for the 'Day of German Art.' Adolf Hitler was expected to visit the city in two days' time. He would declare the festival officially open, and there was to be a reception in the 'House of German Art.'

That was exciting news indeed, a wonderful opportunity, and we decided to make the most of it. Every one of us, of course, hoped to see the Führer. But now the most important thing for us was to find lodgings. That proved to be a real problem. We went from hotel to hotel without success; they were all booked up. We even stopped people in the streets and asked them if they knew anyone who would have us for two nights. It was no good. Eventually we went to the police-station, and the constable on duty gave us a few private addresses. At last we were lucky. Some people were prepared to squeeze us in somehow provided we paid well.

The next morning we went out and started to explore the city a little. None of us had been to Munich before, and as the Führer was not supposed to arrive until the following day we had plenty of time on our hands.

First we had another look at the decorations. They were beautifully done. The town was a charming sight, with the flags on the roof-tops, little coloured-paper lanterns on all the window-sills and lovely flower arrangements everywhere. Huge searchlights had been installed at the Odeonsplatz in order to illuminate the whole Feldherrnhalle by night. This was a most impressive building, with huge pillars and two large lions

in front watching over the peace of the dead inside the hall. A
fire burned in a basin on each side of the entrance. It was
replenished night and day so that it never went out. The two
S.S. guards outside stood absolutely rigid, like statues.

What puzzled us though was that every person walking past
those guards within eight yards raised his hands in the Hitler
salute. This seemed to us to be a somewhat peculiar habit and
when we made inquiries we were told that those who failed to
give the salute were likely to be stopped by an S.S. man and
questioned about their negligence.

Later on we discovered that all the roads which Adolf Hitler
was to take on his drive round the city were lined with large
rostrums. These rostrums were broad and had several rows of
benches on them, arranged as in an amphitheatre. We found
out that the benches had been put there specially for people who
wished to watch the long procession which was to follow the
Führer's drive. A native informed us that we could easily buy
tickets if we wished. They were available at all the paper
kiosks and did not cost very much. The man at the kiosk told
us that the procession would consist of artists, singers and
actors from all over Germany who had come to Munich
specially for the occasion. They would all be dressed up in
theatrical costume, each group representing the cast of some
opera, play or operetta. Some would be posing on carts
covered in flowers and drawn by at least six horses, others
would walk.

It was well after midday by the time we had seen all the
things we wanted to see. Our stomachs were beginning to
rumble and we decided to have lunch in one of the countless
pubs of the great city.

After lunch we went to have a look at the Braune Haus, the
actual birth-place of the National Socialist organization. It
was there that the first five members of the N.S.D.A.P. met
and founded the Party.[1] We found it a large dull building

---

[1] Hitler joined later; he was number seven.

which looked just like any ordinary hotel, except for the fact that two S.A. men stood on guard outside.

We all agreed that a visit to the famous Hofbräuhaus would prove to be a far more interesting experience, and our expectations were fully realized.   There were a few steps and a large wooden door leading into a basement beer cellar, a very large room with huge barrels of beer at the end of it.   Waitresses in crisp white aprons, their plaits arranged on their heads in 'Gretel' fashion, drew the beer for their customers.

The room was ill lit and furnished with coarse wooden tables with benches attached on each side.   Each one reached from one side of the room to the other.   The place was packed and we had difficulty in squeezing on to a bench.   We had hardly sat down when the man sitting next to me began to quarrel with the one sitting opposite.

'What are you staring at me like that for?' he asked, in the broadest Bavarian dialect.

The other man was half asleep, resting his chin in one cupped hand.   He did not stir and we thought he had not heard, but a few moments later we heard him reply indifferently:

'I'm not staring at you, you idiot, you're not worth staring at.'

The fellow on my side jumped to his feet as if he had been stung.

'You call me an idiot,' he bawled, 'insulting me, hey, is that it?   You wait and see.   I'll show you.'

The other blinked up disinterestedly, but suddenly, without any warning, a hard blow hit him right below his ear.   That did it.   Within seconds they were both holding knives in their hands, ready to draw blood.   Some waitresses came running along quickly, trying to stop them.   There was some grappling, a frightened shriek, and one of the waitresses detached herself from the group, her hand dripping with blood.   The girl was led away, and some other customers got hold of the two fighting men and bundled them out of the cellar on to the street.   We had witnessed one of those beer-cellar brawls which are so typical of the Bavarians. They start them just for the fun of it.

Somewhat shaken, we decided that the beer cellar was not exactly the sort of place we would choose for our entertainment and we went to take a look at the room at the top of the flight of spindly stairs. Here there were proper chairs and tables and better lighting. People were coming and going all the time just like pigeons in a dovecote, taking very little notice of the horseplay and brawls that went on unless they happened to get involved themselves.

'Let's go home to bed,' said Father at last. 'It's late already, hardly worth going anywhere else, and we want to be fresh tomorrow. It's going to be a hard day.'

On our way home, in an ill-lit little back street, we passed two middle-aged Bavarian couples. They looked like prosperous citizens out on an evening stroll. Their clothes were immaculate, and each gentleman had linked arms with his respective lady. With his free hand one of them was holding a twin lead; and attached to it were two dachshunds, pulling madly.

By some misfortune the lead got twisted round the legs of the other gentleman and sent him sprawling on the pavement. The first gentleman hastily tried to make amends by helping the other one to his feet, but as both men carried walking-sticks he was rewarded with an echoing blow across his back. He very quietly handed the lead with the dogs on it to his wife, gripped his stick tightly and struck back.

The dogs were barking furiously, the gentlemen were calling each other 'filthy dirt sacks' and all the time the ladies just stood and looked on, completely unperturbed. As soon as the gentlemen had cooled their tempers they turned with stiff little bows to their respective ladies, politely offering an arm, and the two couples walked away from each other into the shadows of the little street.

The next morning we went early to take our seats on the rostrum. At a kiosk we bought little paper swastika flags which we were going to wave when the Führer drove past us. Nothing happened for a long time, but finally, shortly before 11 a.m., we saw Hitler's black limousine turn into the road from the Odeonsplatz. A thunderstorm was brewing and it was unbearably hot. The storm broke just as Hitler came by. A terrific clap of thunder shook the place, the clouds burst open, and within a few minutes we were all drenched to the skin.

I felt a raincoat come parachuting on to my head, and as I looked up I saw a young man standing on a ledge of the building behind us. He was signalling to me, and when I went over he shouted down to me that I could have his coat and give it back later. He would wait for me in two hours' time outside the café at the Rathausplatz. When I returned the coat to its owner the storm had passed and the sky was clear again. Once more the sun had come out.

Hitler was to give a speech in the 'House of German Art' in the afternoon, so we snatched some lunch and got on our way to the famous building. We hoped to see him a little better this time, but when we arrived we found it was impossible to get anywhere near the place.

'I'm going back,' said Father. 'Who's coming? We haven't got a hope in the world.'

I stayed and inch by inch squeezed my way forward into the crowd. The heat was terrific. People were fainting all round me and I watched the victims being carried off by the Red Cross, who had set up their tent on the grass beside the drive. That gave me an idea, and I pretended to be faint too. A woman near me signalled one of the S.S. men cordoning off the square. Within a few moments he had spotted me and worked his way through the ranks of people to where I stood. Without a word he picked me up and carried me to the Red Cross tent.

When he found out his mistake he was rather amused and took me to where I could get a real view of our Führer. The large black limousine was moving at walking pace, and I remember raising my arm, waving and shouting, my heart filled with pride and enthusiasm. Hitler's face was serious. He was standing up in his car, bowing slightly to the left and right at the crowd from time to time, or raising his hand in the Hitler salute. I stood rooted to the ground, staring sadly at his solemn features. What I remember best about him are his strikingly vivid eyes.

All the others were there as well, following close behind in their cars, Hess and Göring, Himmler and Göbbels, and many more.

It was all over in a few minutes, and just as I turned to go I saw my friend from the S.S. standing a little behind me smiling happily.

'Had a good look?' he asked.

'Wonderful. Thank you, thank you very much. That was very kind of you.'

When I got back to the place where we were staying I found Father in deep gloom. Petrol rationing had just been announced. Unless we could find some we would have to leave the cars in a garage in Munich and go home by train. But late in the afternoon, after much bribing, we were on the road again, homeward bound and with our petrol tanks filled to bursting point.

'I knew it,' said Father suddenly into the gloomy silence of the purring car. 'That thunderclap this morning. It was a bad omen.'

3

WAR

The Polish campaign lasted less than three weeks; after that there was stalemate for six months—the 'phoney war.' R.A.F. bombers dropped leaflets over Germany and the Germans had forbidden their aircraft to attack land targets in Britain and France in case civilians should be killed. The Russians attacked Finland in November 1939; the German prison ship *Altmark* was seized by the British in February 1940; and on 9th April the Germans occupied Denmark and attacked Norway. By 3rd May the war in Scandinavia was over. On 10th May the campaign in the West began; the Germans overran Holland and Belgium (though the B.E.F. succeeded in evacuating a large proportion of its troops at Dunkirk), and had brought France to her knees by the third week of June. Apparently no serious preparations for launching a sea-borne invasion against Britain had been made, and when the British, although heavily outnumbered and now alone in the struggle against Germany, refused, under Churchill's tenacious leadership, to surrender or to discuss terms of any kind, Hitler launched a tremendous air attack against them. He hoped to smash Britain's small defensive air force, wreck her port installations, create panic among the civilian population and, by controlling the Channel from the air, make an easy landing within a few weeks. In England it was a time of exceptional tension, courage and suffering on the part of the ordinary people, especially those living in the bombed areas; for the Germans events seemed more remote: only those with relatives in the battle were directly concerned. The battle of Britain opened with attacks on Channel convoys in the first week of July, spread to coastal areas in August and soon after reached London. It died away spasmodically in October; by then the main weight of the attacks had been transferred from daylight to night and was directed mainly at London and other large towns. Air losses were heavy on both sides: but

34

the German losses were the greater, and the failure to crush Britain at this point was Hitler's first major defeat. It was to have incalculably serious results for Germany.

I WAS at school when war was declared. As I came down the stairs from a geography lesson one of my classmates ran up to me, excitedly pointing at the blackboard beside the teachers' rest room. Any special information concerning the whole school was always written on it, and at that moment our headmaster was busy there with the chalk. I stepped nearer and my eyes fixed themselves on the words: 'War has been declared.' The next thing I remember was the anxious face of my classmate who was bending over me and trying to help me up from the floor. It was my first real black-out.

The implications and consequences of those four words must have shocked me profoundly, as I could find no other explanation for my lapse. I should have been happy and proud like the Hitler Youth, elated by the thought that this was Germany's chance to make the process of rehabilitation complete, whereas I was shocked, terribly and deeply disappointed that Hitler was not great enough to avert such a catastrophe. He had achieved a great deal, not by force but by the threat of force, and convinced many of us that he would never take that final step. My father broke down completely. The general reaction amongst the German people, however, was one of elation.

There were different class distinctions now. Germany consisted of ardent National Socialists, moderate National Socialists and indifferent National Socialists. Any opposition had been swallowed up a long time ago. In each category there were about the same number of people from each of the three old classes—working class, middle class and what we referred to as the 'top ten thousand.' I think the Government found that the class most difficult to handle was the old upper middle class.

Their background and upbringing had been one of moderation in every respect. They included the intellectuals of the nation, capable of seeing and criticizing things which other classes were likely to overlook. If this war were really necessary for Germany they were willing to sacrifice their sons, but they were far from sure that it was. By no means were they enthusiastic.

The sons of the wealthy aristocracy were, as always, the first in the country to volunteer. With them it was a question of honour and tradition. They still considered themselves to be the leading class and personally responsible for their country's well-being. To let Germany down at a moment like this would have been treason and a very bad example to those of humbler origin.

For the young people, of course, whatever their origin, part of the attraction was the adventure. German men knew they were good soldiers and felt absolutely confident.

The Polish campaign was over in no time. Germany was proud and reassured when the final victory was reported. There were thanksgiving services in every town and a victory parade was announced. The local troops assembled in the market square with their flags and banners. Several military bands played. Speeches were delivered by high-ranking officers and by our Kreisleiter.

He was a very nice old man, the son of a shoemaker and one of the earliest members of the Party. The Government had rewarded him for his long and faithful service by giving him this job which put him in charge, politically, of the whole population of our town. He was thoroughly honest, kind, and a good disciplinarian as far as the Hitler Youth was concerned. He would stand no nonsense from any youngster and made sure that special rules made at a higher level were strictly obeyed. One of those rules was that all male and female members of the Hitler Youth under the age of nine and in uniform had to be in their houses by nine o'clock at night. Older boys and girls were detailed to patrol the streets, with instructions that if they saw any of the younger children out alone after that time they

Above: The author's home town, where she grew up; the castle can be seen top left, and her home is to the right of this.

Left: The author, eight years old, skating on the frozen lake at her home town.

should take them home and report them to the town head-quarters of the Hitler Youth. Eleven o'clock was curfew for youngsters up to eighteen, and the police dealt with offenders in the same way.

Another thing the Kreisleiter could not stand was disobedience and disrespect on the part of the young towards their elders. In this connection my father one day witnessed an interesting incident. The main road from Gera to Leipzig leads through our town. At one point it becomes very narrow, with a high wall on one side and a row of large warehouses on the other; for two hundred yards the pavement is only about two feet wide.

Father was on his way home late one afternoon when at this particular stretch of road he saw a woman, who was pushing a pram with a baby in it, arguing with two fairly grown-up Hitler Youth leaders in uniform. An elderly man who was passing the group stopped for a moment to listen to what was said between these three people. Suddenly he raised his right hand and boxed one of the boys' ears so soundly that my father could hear the smacks. The two boys were furious, and uttering some threats they hurried away.

What had happened was that the two boys had arrogantly ordered the woman with the pram to get off the pavement and let them pass, as they were in uniform and consequently had priority. It was strictly forbidden to hit youngsters wearing Hitler Youth uniform, and everyone was sure that the elderly gentleman would get into serious trouble for his rash action. The boys were bound to report him to the Kreisleiter.

They did, and the Kreisleiter thoroughly approved of what the gentleman had done. He ordered the two 'leaders' to come and see him and personally reduced them to ordinary Hitler Youth boys because, as he emphasized, they were unsuitable to hold the position of leader any longer. There was not a soul in the whole town at the time who did not admire the old Kreisleiter for his brave way of exacting justice.

D

We were all rather fond of this kind, elderly man, who, like most of those Party leaders, felt it his duty to copy Adolf Hitler as much as possible. Speeches were not exactly his line, but he tried hard and embroidered them with lots of difficult words. He would sometimes give a sentence a different meaning from what he wanted to convey, but I think we all understood.

The victory parade for the Polish *blitzkrieg* was concluded by the 'Grosser Zapfenstreich,' a ceremony which always moved us deeply. It was conducted at all important gatherings and parades. The flags were lowered and the band would strike up very quietly, playing an old well-known church hymn. Both the words and the tune were lovely:

> We praise Thee our Lord Jesus Christ and the power of love which manifests itself in Thee. We promise, O Lord, that this love, which Thou hast brought into the world, will prevail in all our actions and words. Thy name will live in our hearts for ever. We are Thine and joyfully surrender ourselves to Thee and Thy sweet love. Amen.

Every person present joined in the singing of this hymn and we believed what we sang. We felt that we had been ground in the dust after the 1914–18 war by our enemies, shamed and disgraced by the Versailles Treaty, and now God was on our side and our course was the right course. When I look back now I feel that this beautiful hymn was more a parody than a prayer, totally unsuitable to be sung in connection with war.

I was in my last term now, working hard for my school certificate. Most of the boys of our age group had already left school to volunteer for the army. As a gesture of gratitude the Government decreed that they should be given their certificate free without sitting for the examination. Only a few stayed on and we rather despised them. They affirmed that they were preparing for an academic career, but so were most of the others who had put the service of their country first.

The girls too could have their school certificate free, provided they undertook work in offices as civil service clerks to enable the men to be released for the forces.   Most of us went of course, but the new idea did not work as well as the Government had hoped.   Within a few weeks the whole scheme collapsed and we were ordered back to school.

I took the written examination early in January 1940.   It lasted a whole week.   There were only nine of us left, out of a class which had consisted of twenty-four girls when we started grammar school.   The others had all crumbled away one by one as the years passed by.

The oral was to take place a fortnight after the written examination and the final results were to be announced immediately afterwards.   I was so nervous that I hardly slept at all the night before this ordeal.   I knew I had passed easily in most subjects, but my written effort in history did not seem to have satisfied my masters.   The oral would prove how much or how little I knew about the subject.

It turned out to be a nightmare.   A minister of education from Weimar was present, and as soon as I entered the examination room I sensed the atmosphere of nervous anxiety.   All the masters, including our headmaster and the minister, were sitting round a large polished table.   Some of the masters were having little conferences of their own, talking to one another in hushed tones, whereas our headmaster was trying desperately to make conversation with the minister.   But the minister would have none of it.   He just sat there, solid and important like a rock.   My poor masters, how anxious they were to please him! For their sake I hoped that I would do well.

I was told to sit down at the table and take the chair opposite my history master.   I did so, and after a few minutes of heavy silence I saw him reach for Hitler's book *Mein Kampf* which was lying in the centre of the table.   My heart sank, and when he put it in front of me unopened I knew that I should fail.

'Can you tell us,' he said, 'what is written in *Mein Kampf*, second volume, chapter II, page 424?'

I stared across at him, my mind racing through all the 781 pages of the book, trying to remember what was written on each one, hoping that the contents of page 424 would come to me in an inspiration. There were a few sentences or an odd paragraph here or there which came vaguely into my mind, but that was about all. The rest was a complete blank.

I was given five minutes to compose an answer, which never came, and when the five minutes were up I admitted that I did not know. Impatiently my master pushed the book a little closer towards me.

'Open the book and have a look,' he snapped, 'and once you have read the page perhaps you will be able to tell us in your own words what the Führer is telling us in this particular chapter.'

I fiddled about with the book, flustered and nervous, turning the pages over a trifle too eagerly. The result was that I missed the page several times before I finally hit on the right spot by sheer luck. I read a few sentences but found that I was too upset to grasp their meaning. My master then asked me a few encouraging questions, but I bungled the lot. He gave up after that and changed to some general questions about Field Marshal von Hindenburg and the situation in Germany after the First World War. I did a bit better on this, but my previous ignorance brought me down one whole degree in the final report.

When at last they had finished with all of us it was midday, and nine worried girls could be seen sitting in the lobby waiting for the results to be announced. Inside the examination room the masters were having a last short conference. At last the door opened and we saw our headmaster standing there. His face betrayed nothing. Nine pairs of eyes were staring at him questioningly. He nodded and smiled. 'You've all passed,' he said. 'Congratulations!'

He came over and shook hands with each girl, and one by one all the other masters filed out of the examination room and joined him, wishing us good luck and all the best for the future. It was a joyful moment. We had won our first victory in life.

'And now, children, take yourselves away and celebrate,' shouted our headmaster, trying hard to make himself heard above the general noise and chatter.

This was the signal we had been waiting for. With a terrific 'Hurrah!' we stormed out of the lobby, down the stairs and out into the road. Outside our relatives were waiting for us. They too had been anxious and were now delighted to hear the good news. There were hugs and kisses and flowers all round.

And now the actual ceremony could begin. We were going to celebrate our school certificate in a manner which had been traditional at our school for many years. At the kerb six coaches stood waiting to take us on our tour round the town. They had been decorated for us by the girls who were to sit for the examination the following year. Garlands in the colours of the school had been threaded through the spokes of the wheels. The hoods were down and bunches of tulips, mimosa and daffodils had been fixed to them all round the back seats. A hired trumpeter was sitting on each box, dressed up in a fancy uniform, with a top-hat on his head. Each coach was drawn by four horses.

We sat in the first two coaches, and the girls who would now be entering on their last term at school followed in the others as our escort of honour. In each coach there was at least one girl with an accordion. We played and laughed, and the people we passed in the streets waved and wished us good luck. We went to the house of each of the nine girls who had passed that morning, and food, drink and cigarettes were waiting for us in every one of them. When at last by six o'clock in the evening we had finished and the coaches were taking us back to our homes, we were already slightly tipsy and the thought of food made us shudder.

The celebration reception and dinner were going to take place in one of the hotels in the town, and we were supposed to be there at seven o'clock. Somehow I managed to change and with my accordion rushed out of the house in time. Passing my mother on the stairs I planted a fleeting kiss on her cheek.

'Expect me any time between now and tomorrow morning,' I said.

'All right.' She smiled. 'Enjoy yourself.'

All our masters and the headmaster were there when I arrived. The dinner was delicious. Our chairs were grouped round the head of the table and decorated with flowers; they represented our seats of honour. Speeches were made, toasts drunk, there was wine and champagne; and soon teachers and pupils were happily dancing round the floor to the music of an old rickety gramophone which the proprietor had hastily unearthed. We were embracing one another, lamenting tearfully any little misunderstandings we might ever have had, reassuring one another that they were now completely forgotten.

We carried on with our celebration until six o'clock. When I went home the sun was rising and the birds were singing. I was tired and happy. Mother was expecting me and welcomed me with a cup of strong coffee. The carefree time of my schooldays was over. I was grown up now, and soon the adult world would claim me.

A fortnight later my friend Ursula got married. It was a lovely wedding. Both bride and bridegroom were radiantly happy, and as I watched them coming down the church steps after the ceremony I felt jealous. I had forgotten at that moment that Germany was at war and the bridegroom a regular officer. The possibility of sudden tragedy never crossed my mind. I only saw their happiness; their future life as man and wife seemed enviably secure.

Ursula's father, who had given up his practice as a solicitor and volunteered as soon as war had been declared, was there to give the bride away. He was now a captain in the infantry. Her brother, a young N.C.O., was best man. Father and son had brought quite a number of officer friends along, and the sparkling uniforms added to the general splendour of this wonderful day. Five months later, within a few weeks of one another, father, brother and husband were killed in action in France.

Ursula was expecting her first baby at that time and the family's physician strictly forbade the mother and Ursula's two sisters to break the news to her until after the confinement. It was a terrible experience for the mother, and within a few weeks she turned into a haggard wreck with the effort of hiding her own grief and at the same time finding plausible explanations for the sudden lack of letters from the front. It was impossible to keep up the pretence for long; Ursula soon guessed what had happened. They had to tell her, and the shock nearly killed her and her unborn child.

The baby was born that winter. It was a lovely, strong boy, and Ursula took heart again, looking forward to the task of bringing him up and caring for him. She loved the child and clung to him for mental support. The little boy died of a rare bone disease on Christmas Eve the following year, and Ursula became a lifeless, unsmiling statue.

After my official discharge from school I had become what we referred to as 'human material.' R.A.D.[1] was to be the next stage in my life. It was compulsory and there was no escape. It meant living in a camp of huts with about one hundred other girls somewhere in the country. During the day the girls were detailed by their young female leader for work

[1] Reichs Arbeits Dienst (State Labour Service), a forced labour organization, originally intended to absorb temporarily the unemployed, then used to mix the classes and eliminate differences, and finally becoming a sort of wartime labour exchange, directing people to work of national importance.

on the various farms in the vicinity. The work was hard, and the food, which was cooked by the girls in the camp, not too good. I was eager to go, but Father opposed the whole idea strongly.

'As you know very well, my dear,' he said to me one day, 'the N.S. Government want to push up the birth-rate. To speed this process up a bit, you will find that where there is a female R.A.D. camp a male one is not far away. They say this is for entertainment and happy get-togethers so that you can all have a break after the hard work. Quite; but we all know by experience that the entertainment in many cases has been carried a bit too far. I realize that nowadays it is an honour to be an unmarried mother, and of course the Government look after those girls excellently, but I am still a bit old-fashioned. Mind you, I don't believe for one moment that you would allow yourself to be brought into such a situation. However, "a child who doesn't go near a fire can't get burned." '

Father was right. The following day he had a little private talk with the local head of the R.A.D. organization, who was a good friend of his and quite prepared to help. As a result of this conversation I found myself a few weeks later happily installed in a nice bed-sitter at Jena, a student of the local Friedrich Schiller University.

Shortly before I left my home town, however, I got a note from the local head office of the Hitler Youth Organization ordering me to call there at once. It was an unpleasant little note, written in a very unpleasant tone. Something was wrong.

I went the same day and a young girl in uniform showed me coldly into the waiting-room. She disappeared behind a large white door marked 'Bannleader,' from which I knew at once that the young man in charge of the whole organization of the district wished to see me. A few minutes later the girl put her nose round the door and called me in.

The Bannleader was typically Nordic, tall, with a long face, fair hair and a long straight nose. His blue eyes were cold and arrogant. He did not ask me to sit down.

'You are over eighteen, aren't you?' he said, coming straight to the point.

I nodded.

He was sitting on a chair behind a large desk. In front of him on the desk lay a folder with some documents in it. The folder was open, and I could see from where I stood that my name was written on the top sheet in capital letters. He picked up the documents and holding them vertically before him suddenly looked up at me.

'Where is your application to be taken into the Party now as a regular member?' he asked. 'I can't see it here. It should have been handed in immediately you reached the age limit.'

I blushed with discomfort under his stern gaze and tried to think of an explanation. For some time neither of us spoke. The simple truth was that I had hoped I would be able to retire from the organization altogether. My attitude of silent indecision seemed to irritate him, for he cocked an impatient eyebrow at me.

'Well,' I started off rather hesitantly, 'I didn't really want to apply for membership. You see I shall be going away very shortly. I always understood that membership was optional.'

He leapt to his feet, his face flushed with suppressed anger. He had knocked his chair over backwards, and it crashed on to the floor with a terrific clatter. He put both fists on the desk and, leaning towards me across it, started to shout into my face.

'Of all the damned cheek I have ever had from anyone, this is really the limit! Do you know what you are? A bloody shirker.' He turned round and picked up his chair. 'Right,' he said, very quietly now after he had settled himself comfortably again. 'Understand this. If by the end of this week your application is not on this desk, we will make life very unpleasant for you indeed.' He closed the file and put it in his out tray.

'Where are you going, by the way?' he asked, almost non-chalantly.

'University Jena. Teaching profession,' I replied in tele-gram style.

'Oh,' he said, with a contemptuous smile on his face, 'teach-ing. I see. Not much of an example to the young generation, are you? Well, I shall bear today's interview in mind, and if you want to get anywhere with your teaching I should hand that application in tomorrow. That's all.'

I went away in a cold rage, but at the same time I realized that I had no alternative. I did as he had told me, and a week later I was sworn in, received my Party book and badge, and thus became a fully established member of the N.S.D.A.P.

After the Party had got me they started to get busy on my mother, who so far had bravely resisted the pressure brought upon her by the local leader of the women's organization. This lady was very Prussian-looking. She wore her hair parted in the middle and pulled back tightly in a bun on the back of her head. Her features were sharp and hard, her moral reputation not as good as it might have been. One of her deputies would frequently call at our house and try to urge Mother to join, but Mother had no respect for her, and it was of no avail.

After my first term at the university I was ordered to do my 'harvest service.' Most of the farm-hands had been called up now, so every student, male or female, had to spend part of the vacation in helping with the harvest.

I was sent to a large farm out in the wilds of Thuringia. The estate was run by an old mother, her widowed daughter and her mentally backward son. A young village girl of fourteen came every day to give a hand. Every morning at six o'clock an armed German guard would bring two French prisoners of war to the farm, and punctually at six in the evening he would return and take them back to the camp which was only about a mile away.

The two Frenchmen worked on the farm all day with hardly

a break for lunch. They worked quietly and willingly. One of them was an elderly man who hardly ever spoke and I was a little afraid of him. Behind his quiet reserve I sensed antagonism, a deep-rooted dislike for all Germans and bitter resentment at his present status as a prisoner of war. The other was a young fellow, typically French in appearance, very handsome, with dark curly hair, a sharp straight nose, attractive, if rather soft, features and remarkable violet-blue eyes. Both men were tall and physically strong. The way in which they went about their tasks showed clearly that they were accustomed to that type of work. They were efficient and self-confident.

The four of us worked hard all day. I had to get up at five o'clock every morning to tend the cows. Hilde, the young village girl, would join me an hour later and together we would finish washing the milking machine, cleaning the churns and tidying up in the dairy. My next task was to prepare breakfast for everyone. The prisoners would have arrived by then, and the widowed daughter would go outside into the farmyard and give them their orders. After breakfast we would tidy up the house and make the beds.

Lunch was at twelve o'clock and afterwards we girls would usually go out to work in the fields. The prisoners would join us then. There was no guard, no protection, they could easily have run away, or even harmed us two girls had they wished to do so. Nothing of the sort ever happened; their behaviour was irreproachable. They did not speak to us, partly because it was not allowed and partly because their German was not sufficiently good to make conversation. But they talked a lot to each other in their own tongue and occasionally they would exchange a smile or gesture with us.

One day I found Maurice, the younger one, sitting on the shaft of the farmcart looking glum and sad.

'What's the matter, Maurice? You look depressed and fed up,' I said in French.

He stared at me in surprise and then his whole face seemed

to light up. He was smiling broadly and said something in French which unfortunately I could not understand. When he realized that he had drawn a blank his face fell.

'Please speak a little slower and more clearly, Maurice,' I encouraged him.

'Oh, I see.' He nodded and understood at once. Accentuating each syllable, he started off once more and repeated everything he had said in nice, clear French.

'So you speak French,' he said. 'That's a nice surprise. May I talk to you sometimes then?'

'Certainly. I should like to talk to you too, and you must correct my bad French.'

He smiled and shook his head.

'Oh no, your French isn't bad at all, but I shall certainly correct any mistakes you make if you wish it.'

We smiled at each other, a little embarrassed, and neither of us spoke for a little while.

'How old are you, Ilse?' he asked me suddenly.

'Why, I'm turned eighteen,' I laughed.

'You know,' he said, looking me up and down thoughtfully, 'you remind me terribly of my fiancée. She comes from Paris and she looks just like you, only she's a bit older, that's all.'

There was another silence, while Maurice looked out across the country dreamily. I started to feel a little uneasy, hoping that the farmer family were not watching us. Maurice's voice cut across my thoughts.

'You know,' he said, 'I get terribly homesick here at times. We were going to get married this summer. Now I shall have to wait until after the war.'

'Ilse, come in and help with the luncheon,' a voice shouted from the farmhouse. It was the old mother. I smiled at Maurice, who nodded sympathetically, and I walked away.

I had many interesting conversations with Maurice after that. It was a wonderful opportunity for me to practise my

French. Even the other man abandoned his reserve now and again and joined in the conversation.

Eventually I found that my strength was giving out; the work was too hard and the hours too long. I started to feel sick with exhaustion at the end of the day. When I asked the farmer if I could have a little rest each day after lunch, he told me in his half-witted spluttering way that if I wanted to eat I should have to work. There would be no question of rest after lunch.

'What's all this about? What's she want?' cut in the widowed sister, who had come along driven by curiosity when she saw me talking to her brother.

'She wants an hour's rest after lunch every day,' he explained.

The woman stood and gaped. 'An hour's rest after lunch!' she shouted. 'Perhaps you would like me to bring you breakfast in bed every morning as well. An hour's rest after lunch! Well, who ever heard of such cheek!' She shook her head. 'Nothing doing, my girl.'

'I told her so,' the brother said sullenly, and walked away.

'Now listen, my girl,' she said to me. 'If you think we don't know that you are messing about with that prisoner of war you're mistaken. One little word dropped by us in the right place and you've had it. See?'

'How dare you,' I shouted back, livid with rage. 'I'm not messing about with the man, I'm merely practising my French.'

'Practising French, eh? Is that what you call it?' she sneered. 'You'd better work a bit harder and practise a little less French if you want us to send a decent report to the authorities about you here. Is that understood? And no rest.'

I nodded. There was nothing else for me to do now: I was in their hands. They could do me a lot of harm if they wished. Heaven knows what would have happened to Maurice!

I was glad to say goodbye to the farm and its owners when I left two weeks later. My time was over; I had done my duty.

One evening the following winter my mother put a newspaper cutting into my hand.

'Read this,' she said, pointing to an article which was illustrated with the picture of a girl who had no hair on her head.

'They shaved her hair off,' said Mother, 'publicly in the market-place in Weimar because she'd been friendly with a French prisoner of war. Gauleiter Sauckel has made an announcement that this is going to happen to every woman who starts anything with a prisoner.'

'What happened to the Frenchman?' I asked.

'Shot, I believe. Anyway, it tells you in the article. She's dead too, poor thing.'

'Dead? How? What did they do to her?'

'When they had finished with her in the market-place they drove her round the town in an open car for hours and hours. They wouldn't even allow her to put a cap on her head. It was bitterly cold, several degrees below zero. She was dead when they took her out of the car in the evening.'

I stared at the picture in my hand. 'And that's exactly what could have happened to me,' I said.

Mother nodded. 'It might. The people on that farm could have interpreted anything into your harmless relationship with that Frenchman.'

All was quiet now in France, and one automatically wondered 'What next?' Would it be an invasion of the British Isles? Perhaps. There were certainly enough rumours floating around. At the moment it was said Hitler was trying to communicate with the British Government for peace terms. When the Battle of Britain started we knew that he had failed.

After two semesters at Jena and three weeks of actual teaching in a primary school, I felt that I was not really cut out for teaching. I was no disciplinarian and the children evidently knew it. When I told Father that I did not want to go on with it he was terribly disappointed.

'What do you want to do then?' he asked me. 'I had so hoped you would stick to our profession.'

'What I really want to do is to find a good man, get married and have children.'

'Do you really?' There was a little pause. 'Do you think that would be a very wise thing to do at the moment? Don't forget, Germany is at war. You wouldn't want to be a widow at eighteen? There's always that side to it, isn't there?'

'Yes.'

'Well, any other suggestions?'

'Couldn't I stay at home for a little while?'

'If you stay at home, the R.A.D. will get you again. Do you realize that? You won't be home for long.'

'And if you speak to your friend in the R.A.D. headquarters?'

Father nodded. 'I can try, but I doubt if he can do anything this time.'

Father went to see the man and the interview was successful. Instead of being sent away to an R.A.D. camp, I was to do my service with the air force at the local aerodrome as a telephone operator.

4

THE AERODROME

In autumn 1940 the only land front was in Africa, where the British faced the Italians who had now entered the war alongside Germany. In October Mussolini precipitated the next phase of the war by invading Greece. The British promptly occupied Crete and in December shattered the Italian Army in Libya. In Greece the Italians were also defeated. These events decided Hitler to send forces to aid the Italians in North Africa, to bring Bulgaria and Rumania into the Axis, and to invade Yugoslavia and Greece. German troops attacked Yugoslavia on 6th April 1941, and crossed into Greece soon afterwards. British forces which had been landed in Greece in mid March were attacked by considerably superior German forces. On 21st April Greece collapsed. Four weeks later German airborne troops began their assault on Crete, and were in possession by 2nd June. Hitler had already decided to attack Russia next.

RUDI fell in love with me at first sight. I met him at one of the annual dances organized by my old school. These dances were a great attraction to me because usually some of my old crowd turned up, boys and girls of my own age group who happened to be home on leave from the forces or on holiday. There was many a happy reunion.

Rudi was the eldest of four brothers. I knew the family vaguely. His father was a surgeon, a typical Hanoverian, with white hair and brilliant blue eyes, who had settled down in our town and made a fortune by running his own clinic and maternity home.

52

The author at eighteen, immediately after passing her final exam at school, holding a bouquet of flowers presented by her friends.

The author, aged nineteen, during the time she was working as a telephone operator at the aerodrome.

I remembered him well, as he had performed an appendix operation on me when I was a child of nine. Looking at Rudi now across the table where he had joined our crowd, the memory of that afternoon came back to me vividly. I had woken up two hours after the operation and found that my arms and legs were strapped tightly to the bars of the cot. With my senses slightly numbed by the anaesthetic, I started to wriggle and twist violently. My frantic bellows of fright and fury brought the ward sister to my bedside, and she in her turn immediately called up the surgeon, begging him to have a look at the convulsed bundle of rage in case there was something wrong.

The surgeon was Rudi's father and the moment he set eyes on me he seemed to get very angry. He ordered the sister to undo the straps, made a thorough examination of my dressing, turned me a little over on to my right side and gave me a sound slap on my naked behind.

'You are a very naughty girl,' he growled. 'Your straps are off now, but if you keep on twisting and making such a noise we shall have to strap you in again and put you in a room all by yourself.'

I was too drowsy to answer but I remember that he stood there a little while longer looking down at me, and just before he left he patted me on the head and smiled.

Now someone had introduced his son to me. The dance band was striking up for another waltz, and with a formal little bow he asked me to dance. As we danced he told me that he was on a fortnight's leave from Greece, where he was stationed as a corporal of the Alpine Troops, that he loved poetry and hated surgery, and that he could never kill anyone.

'If I fight I fight for Germany,' he said, 'not for Hitler. Hitler's a brute.'

Later on he took me home and proposed to me at the gate outside our house. I begged him to wait a little.

'I'll wait,' he said, 'as long as you want me to,' and we parted

E

with the promise to write to each other regularly.   Maybe on his next leave we could get engaged.

I had almost made up my mind that I was going to marry Rudi when I met John.   I was on night shift one evening in the exchange and someone rang up to ask for the correct time, starting a little conversation.   Half an hour later there was a heavy bang on the steel door of our bunker, a not unexpected call as one officer was on duty all night at the aerodrome and made his round through all the buildings.   When I opened the door there stood a handsome flight-lieutenant, over six feet tall and very fair, with large blue eyes.   This was John.

'Are you the officer on duty?' I asked.

He nodded and smiled.   'May I come in?'

'Certainly.'   I stepped aside at once for him to pass and barred the door after him.   He looked round, undecided where to go next.

'This way, please, to the exchange,' I said, pointing at the half-open door opposite the entrance.

There were two other girls on duty and our supervisor, an elderly lady with white hair, to whom he addressed himself.

'Is everything all right?' he asked.

'Yes, thank you,' she replied, returning his friendly smile. 'We are fine and not at all busy at this hour of the night.'

He nodded and sat down on our chair for visitors.   There was an embarrassed little silence all round and then everybody settled down to a chat.   The young officer seemed quite at ease and told us that he had arrived at the aerodrome only three days before and did not yet know his way about.

'You are the young lady who gave me the time over the phone a little while ago,' he said, turning to me.   'I think I recognize your voice.'

For no reason at all I felt my face flush.   Everybody was looking at me, and the girls were smiling.

The young officer rose and stood for a few minutes studying our duty sheet which gave the names of the girls and the times of our three shifts. Then he turned round, saluted us, and with a cheerful good night left the exchange.

'Somebody here who wants to speak to you, Ilse,' said one of the girls to me suddenly. I had been dozing with my head on the switchboard. I pulled myself up into sitting position and glanced at the clock on the wall.

'Exchange here,' I said sleepily.

'Hallo,' called a cheerful voice from the other end. 'Is that you, Ilse?'

I pricked up my ears. A man, and he was calling me by my Christian name!

'Who's that?' I asked. 'Who's speaking, please?'

I heard him laugh. 'It's me, the duty officer.'

'Oh yes. Do you want the time, sir? It's exactly three minutes after two o'clock.'

'Good Lord no,' he burst out, 'I don't. I want to speak to you. Privately, not officially, and please don't call me sir. My name is John.'

'All right, John,' I said, 'but how did you get to know my Christian name? Tell me that first.'

'Simple. I saw it on the duty sheet. Listen, I shall be on the same bus as you this morning going back to town. Would you mind if I met you at the bus stop?'

'Right oh, I don't mind,' I said, hoping that my voice hadn't sounded too eager.

I put the switch back slowly and removed the plug from its socket, wondering vaguely if I had not made a mistake. These young officers were all alike, cock-sure of themselves and convinced that they were irresistible.

He was there already when I arrived, and during the ride back to town he asked me if I would meet him at a little café in the

centre of the town the following afternoon.   In the café he told
me about his family who lived in Westphalia where they were
rich landowners.   His father worked as an agent for a big firm.
John was an only child, and his education had virtually been the
same as mine.

'Now tell me about yourself,' he said, smiling.   'Come on,
let's have it.'

I smiled back.   'All right.   To tell you the worst straight
away, I'm a schoolmaster's daughter.'

'Oh dear,' he laughed.   'You don't say, so that's where all
the seriousness comes from!'

Then we made another date.

'The afternoon after the day when I have come off night
shift,' I said.

'Now let's see,' he said, puzzled for a moment, 'that would
be Sunday, right?'

I nodded.

'Wonderful.   Sunday then, same time, same place.'

We met frequently after that, and bit by bit we fell in love.
It was an uneasy kind of love, full of teasing, moods and indecision.   One day we would get on very well and be terribly
happy and at the next meeting we would bicker and misunder-
stand each other.   John's moods changed very quickly, and by
now I was so deeply in love with him that his attitude sometimes
hurt me almost beyond endurance.   Several times I decided to
break away, but I never did; I couldn't.

At Christmas 1940 a party was given for all the civilians
working at the aerodrome.   The ballroom of the officers' mess
had been decorated with flowers and there were several large
Christmas-trees with countless candles on them.   Tables had
been laid for two hundred people.

As I stood by the door watching all the coming and going
a tall, elderly captain in Signals uniform came over and asked

me if I would like a drink.   He was our new Signals officer, a
Bavarian, very thin, with heavy bones and sharp, wooden
features.   Then dinner was served, an excellent meal despite
the food rationing, with speeches and toasts and afterwards a
dance.

One of my partners was a young Signals corporal, dark and
rather sturdy, with a pleasant round face, who had been a law
student, and was looking forward to returning to his profession
as soon as the war was over.   Our Signals officer introduced me
to another elderly officer, sophisticated and very intelligent, who
came from Pomerania.

As time went by I became more closely acquainted with those
three men.   They were eager for interesting conversation, and
their keen intellects found no satisfaction in the usual super-
ficial small talk of the officers' mess.   Soon they became
regular visitors at our house.   My father's huge library
attracted them enormously and we spent many happy evenings
at home with my mother and father, discussing books or
exchanging views on current affairs.   Occasionally we even sat
down to a game of cards.

Our Signals officer used to come down to the exchange during
night shifts and sometimes he would sit and talk to me for
hours.   He was a deadly enemy of Hitler.   Life had not
treated him kindly.   His wife was an incurable alcoholic and
his only daughter had run away from home.   He had worked
for a large newspaper in Munich as a reporter, but when Hitler
came his habit of making careless remarks about the new regime
very soon led to his dismissal.

'Of course,' he said to me one night, 'I know perfectly well
that sooner or later I shall end up in one of those concentration
camps.   Not that it matters.   After all I have nothing to lose.
Rather that than make a snakes' pit out of my mind.'

'Surely they wouldn't send you off to a camp just for making
a few silly remarks?' I said, rather surprised at his suggestion.

He laughed rather sarcastically.   'Oh, wouldn't they!   My

dear girl, you'd be surprised who's in those places and what for, if only you could go and see for yourself.'

'You seem to know an awful lot about them,' I said. 'Have you ever been in one? What are they like inside and what happens there?'

He gave me a queer, appraising glance and then he shook his head. 'No, I have never been inside myself, but I knew someone who had. He didn't tell me much, but what he did tell me was unpleasant enough, I assure you.'

Our conversation was interrupted by the familiar 'burr' at the switchboard. It was two o'clock in the morning. This would be the met. office, as the weather frogs were always the first ones to come in for the general time check. All the other departments would soon follow and I should be very busy then. Captain B. knew the routine. When I had finished with the met. office he rose to go.

'Well, my girl,' he said, stretching his long limbs lazily, 'I'd better be off. You'll have a lot of work to do in a moment. But take this from me: in a Germany where Hitler rules everybody has got to howl with the pack; if you don't they'll get rid of you. Hitler is a Bavarian, and I know the Bavarians.[1] I'm one myself. You're a fool to expect compunction from anyone who belongs to that lot. They're completely ruthless, and Hitler is no exception. Believe me, he's a sack, that man, a real bad sack.'

Our captain did not in fact go to a concentration camp, but his provocative remarks soon lost him his commission. One day, without any fuss, he was gone, and another more desirable man was put in his place. We were all sorry that we had lost him. He had been one of the nicest Signals officers we had ever had.

His friend, the officer from Pomerania, had been luckier in life. He was happily married and had two lovely daughters. Just like our former Signals officer, he thoroughly disapproved

[1] Technically Hitler was an Austrian, by a matter of a few hundred yards.

of Hitler, but he was far more cautious and subtle in his remarks. He had been educated at one of the best schools in Germany and taken a degree in foreign languages. To him Hitler was a coarse Bavarian peasant gone wild. How an intelligent people like the Germans could allow themselves to be ruled by an uneducated charlatan passed his comprehension. He was the first person I met who was firmly convinced that Germany would lose the war.

One evening when I came home from the aerodrome Mother told me that a beautiful bouquet of white lilac had been delivered for me. 'From an admirer,' said the little white card attached to the flowers. There was no signature. My heart leapt with joy. I was certain that the lovely gift had come from John. I was soon to find out how badly I had been mistaken.

As I was waiting for the bus to take me to the aerodrome the following afternoon, the young Signals corporal whom I had met at the Christmas party suddenly turned up beside me. We shook hands and talked for a while in a casual, friendly manner, and when the bus arrived we got in and sat down next to each other. Somehow during the conversation I mentioned the lilac and he admitted that he had been the sender. The bouquet of lilac was the beginning of a very pleasant friendship: a friendship which has lasted to this day, even though Kurt is married now and has a family of his own.

Kurt and I went for long walks, and sometimes he came home with me and spent the evening at our house. He too was against Hitler and National Socialism. He hated the army and resented being bullied about and shouted at by officers and sergeants, who in most cases were inferior to him in knowledge, education and background. He loathed the 'upstart policy' which was propagated by the N.S. Government, but realized of course that as Hitler was an upstart himself it was natural for him to encourage it.

He was frank and quite unafraid to express his opinion, and one day the Government caught up on him. He was posted to a penal battalion and sent to the Russian front, but survived and managed to get through to the West shortly after the war was over.

Two days before Rudi was due back for his leave I fully realized what had happened to me since that evening in the exchange when I had met John for the first time. I decided to tell Rudi the truth.

That evening the telephone rang and when I answered it I heard a woman's voice asking for me.

'Ilse is speaking,' I said.

'Oh, I see.' There was silence at the other end for just a moment. 'I'm Rudi's mother, Ilse,' the woman's voice said, 'and I have some bad news for you. Rudi is dead.'

'Oh no,' was all I managed; I had been so totally unprepared for it.

'Yes, it's true, and we will all have to be very brave.' Her voice was trembling with suppressed tears. 'Would you like to come to our house tomorrow afternoon? It would be a great comfort to my husband and myself. Will you come?'

'Of course I will.'

'Thank you very much; that's very kind of you. Come at about four o'clock and we'll have tea together. All right? Goodbye, my dear, and be brave.' She hung up before I could say any more.

A maid answered the door when I called at their house the following afternoon. She showed me into the hall, asking me to wait a moment while she went to inform her mistress. Left alone I felt frightened. I had really no right to be here. I dreaded meeting Rudi's mother. What, I wondered, had Rudi told his parents about me? Would they receive me as a daughter-in-law? If so I should have to play the part well for their sake. It would be inhuman under the circumstances to admit that I was now in love with another man and never really intended to marry Rudi. Somehow I should have to live down this lie and pray that they would never find out.

Someone was playing the piano. I knew the tune well, one of Robert Schumann's *Songs of the Dawn*, a last hymn in praise of the beauty and glory of this world and its creator, written just before the darkness of insanity fell on the composer. All at once I began to cry uncontrollably, and as I followed the maid into the music-room my eyes were blind with tears.

Once inside I stood there, covering my eyes with one hand and sobbing. My grief was so genuine that it seemed to drain me of all my strength, and if it had not been for Rudi's mother I should probably have fainted. I did not know she was in the room until I felt her arms round my shoulders, supporting me and guiding me towards a chair. She did not speak, but occasionally I felt her stroke my hair.

When I had finally calmed down sufficiently I saw her sitting there on the chair opposite me, and she was smiling, forgetting her own grief in her desire to give comfort and tenderness to someone else.

'Poor child,' she said. 'I thought you were going to faint. Do you feel better now?'

'Yes, thank you,' I murmured. 'I'm terribly sorry. I'm afraid I've been a dreadful nuisance to you.'

'Not at all. Don't worry about that,' she said. 'It was quite understandable. And now you are going to have a cup of tea with us. That will soon put you right again.'

The old doctor came in and greeted me cordially. He had not changed at all. Then tea was brought, and when we had settled down Rudi's father told me what had happened.

Rudi had been on his last guard duty before going on leave and had come back into the guard-room to hang up his helmet and his pistol, which hung loosely from its holster on the belt. He must have done this hurriedly because the pistol fell to the floor and went off. Rudi was shot through the spleen and liver. He died almost immediately.

'Did you recognize the song I was playing just before you came in?' said Rudi's mother.

'Yes, I think I did. It's one of Schumann's last compositions. I used to play it myself on the piano.'

She nodded. 'It was Rudi's favourite song, and now that he is gone I play it every time I start to fret because I have lost him.'

Two days later John told me that his posting had come through. He was to continue his training at an aerodrome near Ulm, a town in the province of Württemberg. It was a late afternoon in spring. We had been for a walk round the lake and had stopped at the gate of our house to say good' night.

'Oh well, it's going to be goodbye then, is it?' I said, feeling shocked and sad. 'Will you write to me now and again?'

'I shall certainly phone at night when you are on night shift. I promise you that, but I'm not so sure about writing, darling. I'm positively the worst writer in history. I hate it.'

'All right. Don't forget me then.'

He laughed. 'You look like a little sparrow freezing in the cold, all huddled up and unhappy. Cheer up. But don't fret if you don't hear from me for some time.'

I looked up at him, feeling the tears stinging my eyes. 'How long will some time be, John?' I murmured.

'Oh, I don't know, little sparrow,' he said, a trifle impatient now. 'You know best how unreliable and moody I can be. Please don't bully me. I can't bear to be pinned down, and anyway I don't think it would be wise for us to get too involved. Don't you agree?'

I did not answer, and when he saw the tears he got angry.

'For heaven's sake, Ilse, be sensible,' he said. 'I'm not worth worrying about so much. The safest thing for you would be to forget me altogether. I'm not the right kind of man for you, and I would certainly never make you a good husband.'

'Maybe you are right,' I said. 'I shall do my best to forget you, the sooner the better.'

He looked at me in surprise. 'You are a strange girl, Ilse,' he said, 'and if I said anything wrong I can only tell you that I'm sorry. Would you do me one favour before we part? Would you give me a little souvenir, something you don't want, which I can wear on me as a talisman?'

I looked down at myself, but there was nothing on me I could have given him. 'I'm sorry,' I said, 'I haven't got anything on me, but if you will wait a moment I can run upstairs and get you something from my room.'

'Oh no, don't do that,' he said, shaking his head vigorously. 'It doesn't matter. I just wondered—what about that scarf you've got round your neck? Could I have that?'

I lifted up one corner and looked at the beautiful glossy silk. It was a scarf an airman had given me who had crashed in the Pyrenees. I shook my head.

'I'm sorry, John,' I said, 'you can't have that. It was a present and the man who gave it me is dead.'

One morning at breakfast I found a postcard propped up against my cup on the table. Mother had put it there for me to see the moment I came down. The card was from John, just a formal greeting, telling me that he had settled down well in his new surroundings and asking how I was getting on.

Life seemed a lot brighter that day. I felt like a little ball bouncing along happily on the ripples of a river. Even the aerodrome did not seem quite so dull. In the evening I sat down and wrote him a long letter. It was a mistake; he never bothered to answer it.

5

VOICES FROM SMOLENSK

Hitler had conquered Poland in 17 days, Denmark in 1, Norway in 23, Holland in 5, Belgium in 18, France in 39, Yugoslavia in 12, Greece in 21 and Crete in 13. His military prestige was at its height, despite his failure against Britain. On Sunday, 22nd June 1941, the German Army invaded Russia. The battle of Smolensk ended on 13th August, with several thousand Russian prisoners in German hands. On 18th October another encirclement battle, this time near Moscow, yielded more prisoners. Then it rained, then frost set in. On 2nd December some German troops reached the suburbs of Moscow but were quickly thrown back by the Russians. Two days later the temperature fell to 32° below zero. From then on the war, as far as the Germans were concerned, meant primarily the 'War in the East.' Throughout the winter 1941–2 the Germans were on the defensive in Russia, and suffered a number of serious reverses there; but in the first half of 1942 the German armies resumed their offensive, driving for the Caucasus.

ON THE eve of my mother's birthday there was a sudden commotion at the front door. Someone rang the bell and called my sister's name. It was the telegram messenger from the post office. When he had not found her at home he guessed that she would be with us. Her parents-in-law had come as well for a quiet little birthday celebration, and we all watched my sister anxiously as she tore the envelope open. She read the few lines and her face went very white. Without a word she handed the telegram to her mother-in-law, but the poor woman was in such a state of anxiety that she was unable to read it, and her husband read it for her.

Heinz, my brother-in-law, had been seriously wounded. He had lost one leg and was in danger of losing the other. The telegram came from a well-known military hospital in Munich. My sister immediately went to the telephone, and the long-distance call came through an hour later. Heinz was there and dangerously ill. He was in no condition to receive visitors. His unit had been attacked by enemy aircraft somewhere in the desert near Tobruk. The raid had come so unexpectedly that before Heinz had a chance to dive for shelter a bomb exploded near him, and because of his enormous loss of blood and the seriousness of his injury he had been flown out of Africa the same day. Soon afterwards my sister and her parents-in-law excused themselves and went home, and like little grey mice who have seen the cat we all crept away from the meagre joys of a wartime birthday celebration.

Soon I got a letter from John. I was overjoyed. He wanted to know if I was still working in the exchange, and if I would like him to ring me there now and again in the evenings. I was already on the way to the telephone, eager to speak to him, when my mother warned me not to be too hasty. A postcard would do very well, she suggested, even if it took a little longer to get there.

'You mustn't lose your head now, my dear,' she said. 'He seems a bit unreliable. No good revealing your feelings for him too much.' She was right of course.

A few days later he phoned me. It was ten o'clock at night, and I was on duty at the switchboard. Our supervisor was doing the long-distance lines that night, so she took the call and transferred it to the phone in our rest-room. I was thrilled at the sound of his voice coming through to me so clearly.

'Ilse,' he said, 'I need you. I'm terribly lonely. Couldn't you come to Munich for a few days?'

'Munich? Why Munich? Aren't you somewhere near Ulm?'

'No,' his answer came back, 'I was posted to an aerodrome near Munich two weeks ago.'

'Why do you want me to come, John?' I asked. 'Has anything happened? Are you going away soon?'

'No, no, it's nothing like that. I'd just like to see you again and speak to you. Take a week-end off. I can book a room for you in an hotel if you like, and we can meet.'

'All right, I'll try, but don't growl if it doesn't come off. I'm sure I can fix it with the exchange, but I can't promise anything as far as my parents are concerned.'

I heard him sigh at the other end of the wire. 'Oh, God,' he said, 'I forgot. Of course your dad is a schoolmaster. Well, you'll have to use all the power of persuasion you can muster. Ring me again next time you are on night shift. Now let me see, that would be in four days' time? All right?'

'All right.'

'Fine, good night then, sweetheart. Have an easy night, and just let me tell you that I love you. 'Bye.'

By the time the significance of those last three words had sunk in he had already rung off. I put the receiver back on its cradle and stood there for a moment thinking. If John had really meant what he said nothing on earth would stop me from going to him. But supposing he didn't? I dismissed the idea as unlikely. It seemed that I'd won at last. Turning round, I saw my supervisor standing by the door watching me. I blushed a little, wondering how long she had been there.

'I wasn't eavesdropping, my dear,' she said. 'I just came to see if you had good news, and to remind you that those lines are tapped and private calls strictly forbidden. If I were you, in future I should make those calls a little shorter. It is quite easy for "Luftgau Three" to trace them, you know, and then you might both get into trouble.'

I nodded and promised to be more careful.

'And now the news. What did he say?'

I chuckled. 'He says he loves me, and he wants me to come to Munich and meet him.'

'What's so funny about that?'

'Well, it's the sudden change. You know how he always kept me on a string. I never really knew where I stood with him.'

'And you are happy and want to go?'

'I do. I'd love to see him again.'

'Oh well, let me know when you want a long week-end off and I'll arrange it here with the sergeant.'

When I told my parents about my plan to go to Munich they were not in the least enthusiastic, and I decided that it would be wisest to let the matter rest for a few days. Luckily for me, though, my sister came to see us the same day to tell us that she had had good news from her husband. His condition had improved so much that he was now allowed to have visitors, and she was planning to go to Munich the following week-end. I realized that this was my chance and begged my parents to let me go with her. I told her my story and she backed me up at once. Together we persuaded my parents to let me go. On Wednesday I rang John and gave him the good news. He was delighted. I gave him the address of the hotel where my sister had booked rooms for us, and told him that we should arrive early on Saturday morning.

'You're going to take the night express from Leipzig, are you?' he said.

'Yes, it's more convenient. The trains are not quite so crowded as during the day.'

'Right, I shall call for you at the hotel at 2 p.m. Will that give you enough time to sleep the journey off?'

'Yes. See you at two o'clock on Saturday then.'

My sister and I left for Munich at midnight on Friday in an overcrowded, overheated, completely unlit train. At each station more passengers came aboard, until at last they had to be lifted bodily into the train through the windows.

A high-ranking Party official with his wife had the seats opposite us, and the poor woman was six months pregnant. Half way through the night she suddenly put her head forward into my lap and started to cry bitterly. When I tried to lift her up she vomited all over my new spring suit. The poor creature was terribly embarrassed and the silly husband made things worse by shouting at her. We rubbed some of the mess off with our handkerchiefs. There was nothing else we could do. The lavatories were crammed with passengers and nobody could get at the water taps. When the train drew into Munich Hauptbahnhof we went straight to the hotel, and after lunch I sat down in the lobby to wait for John.

Punctually at 2 p.m. I saw him come through the big swing doors, looking as handsome as ever.

'I suggest a little tour round the shops first,' he said, taking me by the arm and leading me out of the hotel. He seemed cheerful and, clasping my arm firmly, took me from shop window to shop window, pointing out things which he thought might appeal to a woman.

'Come on,' he said, 'you choose something really nice, something you've wanted to get for a long time, and I'll buy it.'

I was shocked. 'Good heavens no, John, I can't do that. Just look at the prices! They're outrageous.'

'Never mind, sweet. Today is my spending day. You tell me what you want and I'll get it. Money doesn't come into it at all.'

We finally settled for a beautiful manicure set in a red leather case which was three times its normal price. We had tea in a little café and for the evening John suggested a variety show. But it was a silly show, and we soon left and went for a stroll through the quiet streets of the big city. It was a beautifully clear night with a full moon, and as we walked along arm in arm, happy and content, the streets seemed to merge into one another, so little did we bother about direction.

The author, nineteen years old, at the time she met John.

'I could walk with you like this for ever,' said John, 'away from everything, especially the war. Sometimes I think that all I want is a little house, somewhere at the Möhnesee, a wife, some kids, peace and quiet and no more flying.'

'You don't really mean that,' I said. 'You could never do without your silly old planes, not for long anyway.'

He smiled down at me. 'Couldn't I?' he said. 'I'm not so sure, you know, Sparrow. Life would be a damned sight more peaceful without them. Perhaps a little pleasure ride once in a while for fun when I feel like it. But not always and every day from morning till night. It gets on your nerves after a time, especially if there is so much to learn and so little time to do it in.'

He stopped and for a little while we stood looking at the moon and stars. When I glanced up at him I thought he looked old and drawn.

'John, what's the matter?' I urged. 'You are not happy.'

He turned and took me in his arms. 'I'm happy at the moment, and I could be very happy later with you, Sparrow, if I'm allowed to live. And that's just it, you see. Shall I?' He kissed me gently on the mouth and we walked on. 'You see, Ilse, I'm really a terrible coward. I'm afraid to die.'

'Die? Why should you die?' I cried. 'Of course you're not going to die.'

'Flying is not a very life-saving profession, you know,' he said, smiling down at me, 'especially during a war.'

We walked on in silence for a long time. A clock chimed somewhere. Midnight. The whole thing was like a dream. Another twenty-four hours, I thought, and I shall lose him again; by Tuesday morning when I go back to work five hundred miles of Germany will lie between us.

'You're dreaming, Sparrow,' he said. 'A penny for your thoughts.'

'I was thinking of you and me and how soon we shall be far away from each other again.'

F

He nodded, and suddenly we were in each other's arms clinging to each other like two frightened children.

'This won't do at all,' said John after some time. 'Come on, darling, I'll take you back to the hotel.' He looked at his wrist-watch and whistled. 'Good Lord, twelve-thirty already. I'm supposed to be back at the airport not later than one o'clock.'

He turned me round and marched me back the way we had come.

' 'Night, sweetheart,' he said outside the hotel, 'sweet dreams and see you tomorrow, same time.'

When he came the next day I noticed at once that he was in one of his difficult moods. He was irritable and made casual flippant conversation. He walked me all over Munich at a brisk pace, hardly ever stopping for a little rest. I followed him meekly. The town was strange to me and I had no idea where we were. My feet started to ache and I was desperately tired. Finally I had had enough.

'Take me back to the hotel,' I said firmly.

'That's the first sensible thing you've said since we met this afternoon,' he answered. 'So far you've just followed me like a pet dog wherever I went, agreeing to everything I said or did. I can't stand girls who have no mind of their own.'

I was so taken aback by this outburst that at first words failed me. Then I was afraid we might end up by having a terrible row, so I decided to leave him alone and shut my mouth tightly. We walked back in silence. I loved him too much to be annoyed, and felt instinctively that this glum, arrogant creature beside me was not the real John. Something was terribly wrong, something that had changed him overnight from a serious, lovable man into a quarrelsome, bad-tempered youth.

At the hotel he took me in his arms. 'Sparrow, I'm sorry,' he said, smiling down at me tenderly. His eyes were asking for forgiveness and I stood on my toes and kissed him on the chin.

'You've got one big fault, Ilse,' he said. 'You love me too much. It frightens me. I'm sorry I made such an ass of myself; please forgive me.'

He bent down and kissed me. 'Goodbye, my sweet. Have a safe trip home. I shall ring you on Wednesday night in the exchange as usual.'

On Monday morning I went to the hospital with my sister. My brother-in-law had just recovered from an attack of jaundice. He looked ill, but said he felt better.

'I'm not going to worry,' he said, 'and when I'm fully recovered I'm going to move and live again, like any other normal man.'

For the rest of that year John stayed in Germany and we wrote and telephoned to each other. Early in 1942, John phoned me one Wednesday night. He said he had done eight hours' flying that day and was dead-beat.

'They're asking a lot of us young pilots nowadays,' he said. 'The training is really hard. I'm expected to have all my certificates by the end of May and after that they'll probably send me to the front.'

My heart sank. 'May. That's only another three months, John. Where do you think you'll go?'

'I couldn't say. That depends entirely on the general situation. We'll be sent where we are needed most.'

'Shall I be able to see you again before you go? Oh, John, I shall die when you're gone.'

'Nonsense,' he said angrily, 'don't be silly. You won't be the only one with a sweetheart at the front. Besides, nothing has been fixed yet. By the way, there's a rumour floating around here about a transfer to an aerodrome near Augsburg. Lechfeld, it's called. If anything happens I shall let you know at once.'

The transfer came through in April and with it John had

reached the last stage in his training. By the end of May the squadron was ready for the front and John asked me to come and see him before they went. A big farewell party had been laid on to which all the girl-friends and wives were invited.

He phoned me on a Tuesday and the party was to take place the following Saturday. I should have to arrive there on the Friday night at the latest, so that I had to get busy straight away. I got my leave, spoke to my parents, who had no objections this time, packed and left on the 2 p.m. express train from Leipzig.

John had phoned to tell me the previous day that he had booked a room for me for Friday night in one of the large hotels at Augsburg, but unfortunately he forgot to give me the name and address. I was not unduly worried about that, as he had promised to meet me at the station. Everything was going to be all right.

It was eleven o'clock at night when I arrived at Augsburg. The air was damp and chilly and there was no moon. A few lamps were burning in the station, dimmed according to black-out regulations, and John was not on the platform. I hesitated for a moment, undecided what to do next, and then I picked up my suitcase and followed the other passengers down the stair-case to the underground passage. I walked up the stairs at the other side and found myself on platform 1 opposite the entrance to the station building with its huge waiting hall. I went inside, hoping that he would be there, but there was no trace of him. The place was almost deserted now. Most of the other passengers who had got off the train with me had left the station. The ticket office was closed. There were no railway officials to be seen anywhere.

The large hall was almost completely dark. I walked over to a bench and sat down, putting my suitcase close against my legs. There was just enough light to read the big clock over the main entrance. Eleven-thirty. Why didn't he come? I glanced at the telephone booth at the other end of the hall. I could ring and find out. I got up, glanced at my suitcase and decided that it would be quite safe there by the bench for a little while.

Suddenly the doors of the main entrance swung open. My heart hammered with new hope, but instead of John three very sinister individuals came through into the hall. One of them made straight for the booth and got in before I had fully realized what he was doing. The other two men were following at his heels, watching me with cunning interest. I stood and stared at them for a moment, feeling really frightened. This was a terrible place. I retreated to my bench and sat down again, making myself as small as possible. Midnight had struck and I was certain by now that John had let me down.

At that moment the sirens started to shriek. There must have been at least two on the roof of the station building, for the noise was terrifying. I covered my ears with my hands and wondered vaguely if I should get up and look for an air-raid shelter.

'Sparrow!'

I was off the bench and in John's arms before he knew what had happened. He stroked my hair and held me close, waiting patiently for me to stop crying.

'My poor little Sparrow,' he said. 'You must have been frightened out of your wits. Relax now, darling; I'm here. I'm taking charge now.'

'What happened? Why didn't you come earlier?'

'It was the air-raid warning that delayed me. Come now, I'll take you to your hotel.'

He picked up my suitcase and with his other hand he pushed me towards the door.

'What about the alarm?' I asked.

'We won't bother about that. They've dropped their bombs about an hour ago. There won't be much now.'

'How do you know?'

'We get all these messages through out there much earlier

than anybody else.   That's why I was late.   As long as they
don't know where the bombers are going to attack, no one is
allowed to leave the aerodrome.'

'I see.'

We ran along the deserted streets.   Above us some aircraft
formations were crossing the town.   We could hear the high-
pitched hum of British aircraft engines, and John even told me
what type of aircraft they were.   He could recognize them
merely by the sound of their engines.

Ten minutes later we rang the bell at the hotel and a night
porter opened the door for us.   He let us enter without
comment and locked the door hastily after us.   At the desk we
gave him my name.   He checked it against the entry in his
book and handed over the key.

'Let's go in the bar and have a quick one before I go,'
said John.   'The lights are still on; they'll serve us if we ask
nicely.'

We had a brandy, and as soon as we had finished we went
upstairs.   John kissed me good night at my door, and I went
to bed.

The next day was clear and beautiful.   I arrived at the
aerodrome just after eleven and John was waiting for me at
the gates.   We kissed and laughed, ignoring all the smiling,
sympathetic faces around us, and then he took me to his billet.
He had a nice little bed-sitting-room, with a comfortable couch,
a bed, a table, chairs, an armchair and a cupboard.   There was
a telephone on his bedside table and a radio on the sideboard.
His room was in a block of prefabs, which served as billets for
all the young unmarried officers.   Directly opposite his window
was a little chapel with a cherry-tree beside it in full bloom.
It was a charming sight and reminded us that it was May.   We
looked at each other and smiled; and then we kissed again and
we both knew that we had never felt so happy before in our
lives.

John had to go out for a little while but came back after an hour, looking strained and worried. He flung his cap into the armchair by the bed and slumped down on top of it.

'Had to come down in a hurry,' he said, leaning back with his eyes closed and trying to undo the buttons of his tunic. 'Port engine caught fire. Damned kite's just been in for repair. Only got her back this morning as airworthy. It's either sabotage or the bloody engineers are no good. This is the third time, and I only just made it. Getting a bit fed up with this, you know. Wonder what the blasted thing will do when I have to fly on my first op. She'd better behave herself then.'

I looked up at him in alarm. 'Oh, please be careful, John,' I begged him. 'Can't they give you another machine, a newer one?'

He shook his head. 'They are new, darling, brand-new. That's just it, that's what puzzles me so. Come on now, old girl,' he said, and pulled me to my feet, 'let's forget our troubles and go for a walk. It's very nice around here, you know. Or would you like to have a look at some of the crates first?'

'Crates,' I said.

'Right oh! Here's your coat. It's draughty on the field. Come along then.'

We went to the tarmac and I had a look at the Me. 110. John lifted me up and I peeped inside the cockpit. The dashboard seemed to be a rather confusing mess of dials, knobs and switches, but I still managed to ask a few fairly intelligent questions about it. Later we had lunch together in the officers' mess and in the afternoon we went for a walk. As we were picking our way through bushes of gorse and heather we heard the planes circling above us, and occasional gunfire told us that some poor chaps were still practising air-to-ground firing. After tea we got ready for the party.

A lot of people were there already when we arrived at the officers' mess. They were standing on the steps of the large veranda in little groups, sipping their drinks and talking. John took me across to the C.O. and his wife. Following the etiquette, I made my little curtsy to the lady and bent low over her hand, kissing it lightly; with the C.O. I simply shook hands. Then we stepped aside tactfully in order to make room for the next guests to be introduced.

John touched my arm. 'Come along, sweetheart,' I heard him whisper close to my ear, 'my wing-commander wants to meet you. He's over there. Let's go and get it over.'

John's wing-commander was a handsome man of about forty. He smiled at me warmly and shook my hand. 'So this is Ilse,' he said. 'I am delighted to make your acquaintance, my dear. The whole squadron will be relieved to know that you have arrived.' He patted John on the back and winked at him. 'You know,' he remarked, turning to me again, 'this young fellow here has been doing nothing else during the last week but talk about his fiancée, Ilse. We were all bursting with curiosity and could hardly wait to meet you.'

I looked at John and saw him blush a little. The wing-commander grinned. 'Never mind, lieutenant, you haven't disappointed us. I must congratulate you on your good taste.'

Dinner was served at seven o'clock. The dining-hall was lit entirely by candles. Two huge chandeliers were hanging from the ceiling, glowing in all the colours of the rainbow. The tables were laid with the best glass and china, the cutlery was silver, and there were flower arrangements on each table. The dishes were mostly Italian, and we all helped ourselves to more. After dinner the gentlemen went into another room for a smoke, while the girls restored their make-up and got ready for the dance.

We danced and laughed and felt carefree and happy. Now and again we sat down and sipped red or white champagne. Half way through the evening John started to flirt with a girl who, according to him, reminded him of a former lady-love, and not to be outdone I started an outrageous little flirtation with one of the other young officers. To my surprise I noticed that John was watching us angrily and seemed to be acutely jealous. Soon after midnight he staged a little unobtrusive scene and urged me to go home.

'Where's home anyway?' I said gaily, still slightly affected by the champagne. 'In your hut?'

'Oh, nonsense. I told you this afternoon that all the girls who don't catch the last train back to Augsburg are sleeping in an officer's empty flat. One of our senior flight captains has given up his flat for the night and moved in with the wing-commander.'

'What about my suitcase though?' I asked. 'It's back in your room. I've got to have it; my night things are in it.'

'We'll go back now and get it and then I will take you to the flat. Come on, let's go. I want to get into bed as soon as possible. I'm dead tired.'

We fetched the case and made our way to the officer's flat. It was a long walk round many corners and most confusing for me.

'What's that?' I asked as we were coming round a bend.

'What?'

'Over there,' I pointed; 'that little red light in the distance.'

'That's a little mock airport. It's meant to confuse enemy aircraft when they come over at night and distract them from the real aerodrome.'

We went on and after another five minutes' walk arrived at a large stone building.

'That's it,' said John. 'I'll go first; I know where it is. Just follow me.'

We went up a flight of stairs and past some doors. One of the doors stood open and we could hear the men on night duty talking. A wireless was playing softly. We went up another flight of stairs and half way down a passage.

'Here we are,' said John, and put the suitcase down. 'The door on the right, over there. I will leave you now. Just go in quietly, in case someone is asleep in there already.'

I got hold of my case, waved to John, pushed open the door and went in.

The room was in darkness. I put my hand to the wall on the left and found the switch. It seemed to be the officer's drawing-room. There was an officer's cap and sword on the table. I walked over and inspected them for a moment, feeling a little surprised. 'I wonder why he left them here?' I thought, and went on tiptoe to the door on the left which seemed to lead into the bedroom. It was ajar, and I stood and listened for a moment. I could hear someone breathing in there, and an empty bed stood clearly outlined against the wall at the far end of the room. The window was wide open and the black-out blind up. I quickly shut the door, wondering if anyone could have seen the light coming from the drawing-room.

There was something very fishy about the place, but I was too tired to care now. I undressed quickly, and after turning off the light in the drawing-room slipped into the empty bed in the room next door. I put my little electric torch under the pillow and fell asleep almost instantly.

A few moments later I sat up in bed with a start. A noise had woken me, but I could not remember what it was. I peered into the darkness, listening. There it was again, a terrific snore and very heavy breathing. It was very unlikely that a lady would make a noise like that, so I snatched my torch from underneath the pillow and walked over to the other bed. I directed its beam on the upper part of the bed and found myself staring into the bloodshot eyes of a man.

'Switch that bloody light off,' he growled. I obeyed at once. His breath smelled horribly and I concluded that he was pretty tight.

A gust of cool air came in through the open window. I shivered and realized that I was standing there dressed only in my flimsy nightgown, entirely at the mercy of a wild, drunken, strange male. As the truth came home I hitched up my nightgown and fled. I banged the bedroom door shut, found the key in the lock and turned it. That was that. It had taken me only a few seconds. If that rascal in there did not go mad now and start banging at the door I should be fairly safe. I dressed hurriedly, putting on every garment inside out, grabbed my case and departed.

All was quiet inside the flat. Now for the stairs. The wretched things creaked abominably as I tiptoed down, pausing every few seconds to listen. The door to the guard-room was shut, but I could still hear the men talking. At the second flight of stairs my last drop of courage left me. I took a flying leap and dived for the main door. My suitcase bumped heavily against the banister, and the door shut behind me with a bang that made the building tremble.

I slipped round the corner and hid under a hedge. All stayed quiet. They must be used to that sort of thing here, I thought, genuinely surprised that nobody was following me. I waited a little longer and then started on the long walk back to John's room. I nearly got lost on the way, but the mock airport and the little cherry-tree by the chapel guided me safely to the prefabs.

The door to John's room was unlocked. I slipped in and switched on the light. He was sound asleep, with his face turned towards the wall. I landed a hard slap on the place where his behind lay outlined on the blanket.

'What's up?' he said, sitting up in bed, looking terribly stupid. 'Where the devil have you come from at this time of the night?'

'Morning, dear,' I reminded him gently. 'I've slept in a room with a strange man.'

I told him the whole story, and he helped me to make up a bed on the sofa. Within minutes we were both sound asleep.

After breakfast on Sunday morning John went out to make inquiries about the previous night.

'Aren't we innocent little angels!' he said when he came

back. 'That story about the vacated flat was just a fake. No one expected the ladies to go there and the captain never even moved out.'

'Who told you?'

'The wing-commander; and he told me something else.'

'What's that?'

'Sit on my lap and I'll tell you.'

Together we settled down in the big armchair and John put his arms round me.

'If I asked you, Ilse, to spend the night with me here in my room,' he said, looking up at me, 'what would you do?'

I stroked his hair and kissed him on the nose. 'Why, John, I should say yes of course.'

'Do you really mean it?' he said, hugging me hard.

'Yes, I do. I love you so much, John, I don't care what happens.'

He pushed me off his knees and got up. 'Nothing will happen,' he said a little brusquely, 'nothing at all. It mustn't and it won't. I promise you that.'

'Why not?' I challenged him, feeling hurt and rejected.

'Because it's madness, absolute madness!' he shouted. 'I wish I had never suggested it.'

'Why are you so angry all of a sudden?' I asked. 'What have I done, John?'

'Oh, nothing, Sparrow, nothing at all,' he said lamely. 'I'm sorry I flared up like that, but you must try and understand. I'm not an experienced lover, if you know what I mean. You might have a baby and what will become of you if anything happens to me? It would be a terrible shock to you and to our parents.'

'No it wouldn't,' I replied stubbornly, 'not to me anyway. I'd love a baby, with golden curls and blue eyes and a big potato nose like yours.'

'Oh, stop it,' he said, gripping me by the shoulders. 'This is a serious business. We're so young, and you especially are too young to have your whole future messed up. Don't you see?'

'But why are you so sure you will die, John? It's terrible, this pessimism of yours.'

He turned away from me and put his cap on. 'Never mind, Sparrow,' he said. 'Come on, let's go for a walk and air our sorrows. We'll decide what we are going to do when we come back.'

During the walk John proposed to me and suggested that we should send a telegram to our parents and let them know about our engagement. We went to the officers' mess, phoned the message through to the exchange, who promised to pass it on at once, and then went into the bar for a little celebration drink. At ten o'clock we returned to John's room and got ready for the night. No more had been said between us on the subject and now it was too late for me to go back to Augsburg and sleep in the hotel.

We made up the bed for me on the couch and soon afterwards we switched off the light, undressed in the dark and got into our beds. I lay awake for a long time. There was no sound from John's bed; he seemed to be asleep. I dozed off at last and was awakened by the light from John's bedside lamp. John was sitting on the side of the couch looking down at me.

'You look terribly sweet when you are sleeping, sweetheart,' he said, smiling affectionately. I sat up and put my arms round my knees.

'What's the time, John?' I asked. 'Have we got to get up yet? Is it morning?'

'Dear me no, it's only just after midnight. I couldn't sleep and I thought we might talk for a bit.'

I nodded and then he put back the blanket and lifted me up in his arms.

'I want you near me tonight,' he said, and carried me over to his bed. 'We're too good really; it's silly, don't you agree?'

As an answer I put my arms round his neck and pulled him

down beside me and for a long time we lay there quite still in each other's arms, absorbing each other's nearness.

'I've been beastly to you at times, Sparrow,' said John suddenly, raising himself on one elbow and looking down at me. 'I'm terribly sorry about that. I wish it had never happened now that I know how much I love you. But I was so harassed all the time. Our training was so difficult and they drove us like mad. Sometimes I thought I would crack up. Even now I feel I haven't grasped it all. It needs hours and hours more of practice and I suppose I'll get that by flying on ops. It's the only way to get the practice in, but I'm frightened. Lack of practice means more casualties, and I know that I'm going to be one of them.'

'Oh, John, there you are again,' I said, and sat up. 'This terrible defeatist attitude. Why should it be you who gets killed?'

'Why shouldn't it?' he asked, shrugging his shoulders. 'You can also put the question that way.'

I shook my head. 'No, darling, I think you are making a mountain out of a molehill. Everyone gets that feeling before going to the front.'

'It's not just a feeling. I know I won't come back and I'm scared of what the end is going to be like.' He lay down on his back and looked up at the ceiling. 'You know, it seems strange to think that there'll be darkness all the time, and I won't see the sun any more, or the flowers, or you—especially you.'

'Oh, stop it,' I said, shaking him hard. 'This is cruel, and you are asking for trouble. Do you want to die? One could almost believe that you do.'

He looked up at me for a moment, and then to my horror I saw his eyes fill with tears. He flung back the blanket and jumped out of bed. Then he put his dressing-gown on and started to pace the room, struggling for composure.

'Come here, John,' I pleaded with him. 'Please, it's all

right. If this is really our last night together, then I want you to love me properly. I want to spend it as if we were man and wife.'

He came over to the bed and stood there for a moment looking at me and then he shook his head. 'No, we're not going to do anything of the sort. I told you why this afternoon, didn't I, or was it morning?'

'Morning,' I said. 'But why are you so stubborn? It's my life, isn't it? And I don't mind. I want you, John. Don't you understand?'

'I do, but that still doesn't give me any right to mess up your life. Look, let's be sensible and wait a bit. If I get through the first few months, then I feel I'll be all right, and on my next leave we can get married straight away and do everything properly and with all the trimmings. I want it that way. It's much nicer and not so messy.'

'You know, I don't think you really love me very much,' I said, 'or you would react quite differently.'

'Nonsense. It's because I love you that I want to have everything done the right way, and anyway it's the way it should be done. Move over now, Sparrow, I'm coming to bed and you are going to be a good girl. Don't make things too difficult for me. There's a limit even to my self-control, and I'm pretty good. You are a very wicked girl really. What do you think our parents would say if they could hear you suggest such immoral behaviour?'

He laughed, and I was glad that the dark mood had passed. Everything seemed all right again, and I felt certain that he had been under the influence of a quite natural depression, known amongst soldiers as front fever. I turned over, and he curled round me at my back and lay there like a shell round a pea. The warmth and nearness of his body comforted and soothed me, and with a feeling of utter contentment I soon fell asleep in his arms. The next morning he came with me to Augsburg to see me off.

' 'Bye, darling,' he called up to me; I bent down from the open carriage window and we kissed for the last time. The train was already moving, and I waved until the platform had disappeared from sight. I pulled up the window and then the tears came streaming down my face.

'Why you cry so much?' a voice asked next to me in broken German. I looked up and saw an elderly Japanese in civilian clothes watching me rather anxiously.

'My fiancé,' I said, and swallowed. 'He's going to the front next week, and we've just said goodbye. I'm afraid I might never see him again.'

The Japanese moved a little closer and put one arm timidly round my shoulder.

'All men must fight,' he said. 'Men are meant to fight and —to die. We all die one day, some sooner, some later. If he die you will meet him again in other world. But now you must be brave. Those from other world, who are dead, will watch you and see you cry. That is not good. As long as you live you must live for life and be happy. It is your duty. And you must cry only a little once in a while perhaps, but very, very little.'

Soon afterwards, as John had anticipated, the second Russian campaign began. He phoned me one Tuesday evening at home. He told me that the squadron was leaving on Thursday night. It would be their duty to support the ground troops in their advance by attacking the Russians from the air first.

One evening I was seated at the exchange at the long-distance section. It was 10 p.m. and the switchboard was beginning to quieten down. There were three girls and one supervisor on each night shift, and two of the girls were now getting ready to turn in for the first part of the night, while the supervisor and I looked after the exchange. Those girls would sleep until 2 a.m. when they took over from us so that we could

John at the time the author met him. They exchanged this
picture and that facing page 69. He is wearing the uniform of an
Oberfähnrich, just previous to being commissioned as a lieutenant.
The four birds on the lapels of the tunic are pilot's 'wings'; the
small badge on the left breast pocket is the insignia of a glider pilot.

have a sleep. There were two comfortable army beds in our rest-room and we had worked out this little system which gave us all a chance to snatch four hours' sleep during each night shift. This particular night I stayed up with our supervisor for the first part of the shift.

Private calls were of course strictly forbidden, but we did get them very late at night when the lines were not very busy. It was a quarter to one in the morning when the red light came on on one of the long-distance lines.

'Aerodrome A. here,' I announced myself and waited. There were a lot of crackles and background noises and then I heard a voice come through, very faint and distant.

'This is Smolensk! Aerodrome A., can you hear me? This is Smolensk.'

'Aerodrome A. here, I can hear you, Smolensk. Who are you calling?'

'I am calling your local number 1028. Can you connect me?'

'Is your call private or military?'

'Private.'

I switched off and turned to my supervisor. 'A man calling from Smolensk, private, local; shall I connect?'

'Smolensk, good God!' She looked up at the clock. 'Ten to one. Nothing should be coming in yet. I think we should connect.'

I went back on the line and heard him shouting at the other end. He thought he had lost me. I announced myself again and he calmed down. I told him that I was going to connect and dialled the local number. I waited, and after a few seconds the sleepy voice of a woman answered the call.

'This is 1028, who's there?' she said.

'This is the aerodrome, madam. You are wanted from Smolensk. Will you please hold the line while I call the subscriber.'

'Thank you,' she replied, sounding a lot livelier already. 'I'll hang on.'

G

'Smolensk,' I shouted. 'Will you go ahead, please. You are connected.'

I put the switch back and laid my earphones down. 'I only hope they can hear each other,' I said.

Our supervisor nodded. 'It would be a shame if they didn't. Hell of a distance that. The longest we've ever had.'

I nodded and turned back to check up on the connection. The white light underneath the local lines was blinking frantically. I slipped on my earphones.

'Operator'—the woman was in tears—'I can't hear a thing. Only crackles. Who's calling me? Is it my husband? He's at Smolensk. Could you find out, please?'

'Just a moment.' I transferred her to a dead line and went over to long distance.

'Smolensk,' I shouted, 'are you there, Smolensk?' Suddenly the crackles were back and I heard another operator shout further down the line: 'Smolensk, you are still connected. I'll ring through again to aerodrome A. Will you hold the line, please.'

'Aerodrome A. here,' I called. 'I've heard you. Will you please put me through to the caller in Smolensk: the subscriber is waiting.' I heard a click and we were connected.

'Smolensk,' I shouted, 'the lady can't hear you. Can I pass a message, please?'

'Yes'—the voice came through very faintly—'if you would, please. Tell my wife I wish her many happy returns of the day. I wish I could be with her. Tell her not to worry, I'm fine. Give her my love. I'm thinking of her all the time.'

I passed that on, and told the young lady that unfortunately the conversation would have to be conducted that way as the lines were too bad to make a direct call possible.

'All right,' she said, a little disappointed, 'thank you very much. Give him my love. Tell him I'm missing him terribly and I do so hope he'll come home on leave soon.' She stopped for a moment. 'What else can I say, operator?' she suddenly asked me. She was crying again.

'Don't cry, please,' I said. 'I'll pass this on first. If you can think of anything else, let me know. I'll be back on your line in a jiffy.'

Unfortunately we had to break it up just then. Smolensk exchange came on to the line urging us to finish. The girl was heartbroken when I told her.

'Don't be so unhappy,' I said to her. 'He might be able to call again some other night on a better line. Good night now, and many happy returns from all of us here.'

She gave a choky little laugh and told me they had only been married five days when he had been posted to Smolensk, and she had not seen him since.

After that for some time private calls from Russia came through more frequently at night. We always connected them. Some of the messages passed were more prosaic than the ones from Smolensk; for example:

'Send me my sweater with the long sleeves, long underpants and more thick socks. It's cold here.'

One night a son called his mother. I had made the connection, and this time they could hear each other very well. There were occasional bursts of noise at his end which sounded like distant shell fire, but apart from that the line was beautifully clear.

'Mum,' he shouted, 'how's Liz? Has she come out of hospital yet?'

'No, not yet,' replied the mother. 'Coming out next week. How are you, Werner? Are you all right?'

'I'm fine, thanks, but tell me, Mum, did she have a very bad time?'

'Who?'

'Liz.'

'Oh, stop worrying, son; she didn't have a bad time and she's quite all right. I'll tell her you've phoned. Now tell me, where are you?'

'Can't tell you, Mum, advanced post, near the front line. Corp. gave me permission . . .' The line faded and I was wondering if I should do something about it when I heard his voice come back once more. Ten minutes later, when I went on to the line for a routine check-up, they were still talking.

6

MARRIAGE TO A DEAD MAN

At the turn of the year Pearl Harbour had brought America into the war on the side of the Allies; but her strength was not yet deployed in Europe.   Indeed she was still on the defensive, being driven from island to island by the Japanese in the Pacific. Similarly for Britain disaster followed disaster, with Malaya and Singapore lost, Tobruk fallen, and the Mediterranean and Pacific fleets put virtually out of action.   Everywhere the Axis seemed triumphant.   At the beginning of the summer of 1942 the Germans were still advancing in Russia, but they were encountering increasingly effective opposition, and losses on both sides in men and material were enormous.   On 23rd October the battle of El Alamein began.   On 8th November the Allies landed in North Africa.   The Russians were still calling for a 'second front—now.' The Japanese Navy had been defeated at Midway.   The battle of Stalingrad was in full swing.   By the first week of February 1943 it was over and the German Sixth Army had been wiped out.

ONE day in July a letter arrived from John.   He wrote that he had settled down well and was not going on ops yet.   His group-captain wanted him at H.Q. and had made him his adjutant, as he thought that John had a good brain for tactical matters.   It was an honour of course and promotion to the next highest rank would soon follow, but personally, he said in the letter, he would prefer to go out with the gang.   I cried with relief when I read it.   For the moment at any rate he seemed to be safe.

One morning a week later Mother brought in a letter and gave it to Father.   We were having breakfast, and after he had looked at the handwriting Father put the letter on one side and continued eating. I poured out another cup of coffee for myself, paying no attention, and sipped the hot drink absent-mindedly, following my own trend of thought. I saw Father turn the letter over and glance at the back where the sender usually put his name. He stopped short, frowned and glanced at me across the table.

Later on he rose and went out of the room, taking the letter with him. Then I heard him call for Mother. I finished my bread and butter, and was just getting ready to catch the bus to the aerodrome when my parents called me into Father's study. They were both looking terribly unhappy and I wondered vaguely if it might have anything to do with the letter.

'I've got a letter here from John's parents,' said Father.

'That's very nice of them,' I replied. 'What does it say? Are they all right?   Have they heard from John?'

Father nodded. 'They have, and the news is not very good.'

I stared at Father and felt my heart go cold.

'What's happened?' I asked very quietly. 'Is he dead?'

'They don't know yet.   He's been reported missing.'

'But he wrote that he wasn't going on ops only a few days ago,' I cried in despair. 'How could this have happened?'

'He went just once, and didn't come back, dear.   It's all in this letter.   Perhaps you would like to read it yourself.   Please, darling, don't lose your head, don't panic, it's by no means been established yet that he was killed.   He might have been taken prisoner.'

Father handed me the letter and I read:

DEAR SIR, I have written to you because I think it would have been too much of a shock for Ilse if I had sent the letter to her. I trust you will break the news to her as gently as possible. Our son John has been reported missing, believed killed.   His plane was last seen over territory which is still in Russian hands. It was flying level at an altitude of less than three hundred feet. The port engine was on fire and the plane was leaving a trail of smoke and flame behind as it disappeared in the distance.

There was very heavy anti-aircraft fire from the enemy at the time and it looked as though the pilot was trying to get the machine away from it, looking for a safe place where he could bring her down.

The rest of the letter was formal and hardly mattered. I folded it and handed it back to Father. Without a tear or another word to my poor worried parents, I left the study, walked out of the house and went down the road to catch the bus to take me to the airport.

As the day wore on I found it more and more difficult to concentrate on my work. Reaction was setting in, and I felt relieved when it was time to go home. Mind and body were aching with the effort to accept the destruction of my happiness, for by now I felt certain that John was dead. In the days that followed, my suffering was so acute that at times I could see my parents shy away from me, baffled by the finality of this cruel blow.

Then John's parents rang up and asked me to go and stay with them for a time. I gladly accepted their invitation and my parents urged me to go soon, hoping that a change of atmosphere even for a little while would restore my lost balance and bring me back to this world, which at the moment I seemed to hate. The journey took me five hundred kilometres across Germany, and as the train drew into the station at eight o'clock in the morning I saw them at once. They were standing under the big clock on the platform. I couldn't have failed to recognize them. John was so obviously their son.

I picked up my case, opened the carriage door and got down. John's mother scrutinized me for a few seconds, then turned to speak to her husband, nodding several times in my direction. Then they both came over to welcome me. Outside they took me between them and, as if it were the most natural thing in the world, I slipped my arms into theirs.

We had to walk home, as their car had been requisitioned by the Government long ago. It took us about fifteen minutes, and they chatted away, pointing out particularly interesting features and buildings in the beautiful old Westphalian town where they lived. In their company I felt myself relax. It was as if I had come home, home to them and John.

The big old house was beautiful. It had been in the family for over two hundred years, and when John's parents inherited it they had had it modernized. I was given John's former bedroom and for the first few days his mother brought breakfast up to my bedside every morning. It was a cheerful room, all in white, and I was happy in knowing that it had formerly been John's and that I was occupying the bed in which he had slept for many years.

John's parents soon asked me to call them Father and Mother and presently they started to introduce me to all the members of their families. There were two sisters and one brother on the mother's side, and four sisters and one brother on the father's. Most of them owned large farms and food was plentiful. Even though a large proportion of all agricultural produce had to be handed over to the Government for distribution amongst the population, there was still enough to spare for the family, and my mother-in-law's larder was well filled with things that were scarce and difficult to obtain.

Westphalia is an agricultural country, and the rich farmers are the ruling class. They are very fond of money, and like to make sure that none of the wealth they accumulate will stray outside the family. Intermarriage is therefore common, with of course its attendant evils: tuberculosis, epilepsy, mental deficiency, physical deformities. Many of the Westphalians, however, are strong and healthy. They are a proud race with a high standard of living for all classes, and, in spite of their generally materialistic outlook, individually kind-hearted and generous. They are slow in temperament and cunning rather than intelligent. In appearance they are typically Nordic: very tall, strongly built, with flaxen hair, strong regular features and blue eyes. With them religion is more a class distinction than a belief, the landowners and upper middle class Protestant, the humbler classes Catholic.

One morning my parents-in-law called me into Father's study for a little conference.

'There was a letter amongst John's things,' said Father, who was sitting in his chair behind the desk. 'We found it in the suitcase which his unit sent back to us a little while ago. It's addressed to us and he wrote it five hours before he was going on his first op. The letter never got posted of course.'

I sat down slowly beside Mother on the sofa, wondering what they were trying to tell me.

'John asks us to look after you and care for you, just as we cared for him when he was still alive. We were going to do that anyway because we both love you very much, but there's one way in which we could help you even more. It's a rather strange thing we have in mind. You've heard about these new government regulations for marriages after death, haven't you, Ilse?'

'I have indeed.'

'You realize, of course, that they are mostly meant for those girls who are expecting a baby by a man who has been killed in action before marriage could take place?'

'Yes.'

'Well, this does not apply in your case, but we think that if you were willing we could try to get such a licence for you. We would like you very much to bear John's and our name, and apart from that it would put you on a very sound financial basis.'

'How?'

'To begin with, as John's wife you would be entitled to draw a pension. As John was in the air force it should be fairly high. Then war widows get all their training free. No matter what you want to do or learn, even university training would be free for you. And there are many other advantages which I have forgotten at the moment. Does the idea appeal to you at all? Please be quite frank. We shall not be offended no matter what you decide.'

'I'd love to do it, Father, but I don't know what my parents will think of it. I'm not twenty-one yet, and I suppose I should have to get their permission.'

'Quite right. Now don't let's worry about that at the moment. Let's get all the documentary stuff straight first.'

He took a bundle of documents from a drawer and pushed them across the desk.

'Here, have a look at those. There's a lot of paper work to be done, but I can help you to fill in all the details.'

I sat and studied the documents for a long time and realized that it would be by no means easy to get permission for a post-humous marriage. As I had expected, my parents were dead set against the whole thing, dismissing it as morbid and unnatural. In the end, however, they gave in.

Soon afterwards my parents-in-law started to encourage me to go out a little more and meet people of my own age. They did not think that it was healthy for a young girl to keep herself locked away, never meeting anyone. They told me that John himself had loved life, and that if he were still alive he would certainly not approve of this attitude. It was now that they introduced me to Irma.

She was four years older than I. Her parents owned the only music shop in the town. She too had lost her fiancé and so knew exactly how I felt; we put our miseries together and soon became firm friends.

Irma was chairman of the local sailing club whose members did their sailing and training on the Möhnesee, some eight miles from the town and easy to reach by train. She owned a canoe, and on Saturdays and Sundays we would go along to the Möhne and spend the day in her boat on the water, with the little portable gramophone perched dangerously on its bow. She had a wonderful collection of records, and while she did the paddling I kept the gramophone going. Those were wonderful days, full of sunshine, peace and nostalgic daydreaming.

Irma also sang in the local church choir, and as I had always been a good singer myself I soon joined her there. On some Sundays she played the organ in one of the local churches for the morning service, and finally she started to teach me this most enjoyable art. At the end of that summer my parents-in-law asked me if I had made any plans for my future.

'You'll have to do something, Ilse,' they said. 'You don't want to stay at the aerodrome for ever.'

They were right of course.

'Why don't you go back to the university?' suggested Father.

'Back to the university—whatever for? To become a teacher like my father? Oh no, I wouldn't like that. I've had a go at that once before. I'm not going to do it again.'

'Who said anything about teaching?' asked Father, a trifle annoyed. 'Couldn't you study something else, something you'd like better than teaching?'

'I don't know.'

'For heaven's sake, Ilse, stop being so vague. Pull yourself together. You've got to think of something. John would be disgusted to hear you talk like that. What do you think about medicine? You said to me once that you would have liked to become a doctor, didn't you?'

'That was years ago, Father. I've given up all thought about it a long time ago. Anyway, it's too expensive.'

'Don't be ridiculous. It isn't, not for you, not once the marriage comes through. Your training would be free. That leaves only the living expenses and books and instruments. Your pension would cover them, and if it didn't we could always help a little.'

I thought this over for a while. 'I should like to be a children's doctor, Father. I love children. Yes, I think that would be nice. Which university do you suggest?'

'Plenty of time to worry about that. Come along now to the

study, and before you do anything else you're going to ring your parents and tell them.'

My parents were delighted when I told them about my decision, and they suggested at once that I should go to the university of Leipzig, a city about twenty-five miles from my home town.   It was already the end of August so I was to begin my training the following spring.

September came, warm and beautiful.   We went to the Möhnesee almost every day, swimming, sun-bathing and canoeing.   One day Irma introduced me to a young man whom I had not seen there before, though I had met most of the members of the sailing club.

'Come and meet Frank,' said Irma.   'He's one of our oldest members and just on leave.   He's a V.I.P. here in our modest circle, you know.   He's got the Knight's Cross!'

'Oh, Irma,' said Frank, blushing a little, 'have you got to tell everyone?'   He turned to me and made a formal little bow.

'How do you do,' he said, rather stiffly.

'How do you do, Frank.   My name is Ilse and I'm actually a stranger here.   How did you win your Knight's Cross?   I'm most interested, or would it take too long to tell?'

'Too long to tell,' he said and smiled, 'and not very interesting.'

Some more members arrived and shook hands with us, and after a few minutes of general polite conversation we all got into our boats.

I went with Irma in her two-seater as usual.   Frank was on his own.   Most of the time the whole party stayed together in a cluster of canoes, with an occasional swim, followed by a rest in the warm sun on the shore.   Half way through the afternoon Frank complained that he was lonely and asked Irma if she would lend me out to him as a partner for a little while, so with much wobbling and splashing I climbed across into the back seat of his canoe.   Immediately he began to paddle away from the rest of the party at a furious pace, ignoring completely their cheers and the jokes they were shouting after us.

'Can't we stay with the others, Frank?' I said.

'No, I would rather talk to you alone,' he replied. 'Let's go up there.' He pointed to the shore. 'There's a very nice little café with a good view. You wait and see.'

We sat down by the window of the large veranda which over-looked part of the huge artificial lake.

'Coffee?' asked Frank.

I nodded.

We sat and sipped, and for a moment he regarded me thoughtfully from across the table.

'You're nice, Ilse,' he said suddenly, 'the nicest girl I've ever met and I want to get to know you quickly. I've only got three days left of my leave. Hence the hurry.'

I shook my head. 'It's no good. My fiancé was killed in action only two months ago. I don't want any men friends yet.'

'You're going to marry him, aren't you?'

'Who told you?'

'Someone did.'

'I hate gossip.'

'So do I, but this isn't gossip. It's true, isn't it? You are going to marry a dead man?'

I nodded.

'Why?'

'I don't know. It's a purely emotional thing. In a way I wanted to help my parents-in-law. If they can't have their son they can at least have a daughter. On the other hand, if you have loved a person as I loved John, it gives you a feeling of satisfaction and comfort that even though he has been taken away from you physically you have nevertheless managed to become his own by name and—spiritually, if you like.'

Frank thought that over. 'It's crazy nevertheless,' he said at last, 'crazy and unnatural.'

'Who's got a right to judge?' I retorted tartly.

He smiled at me apologetically. 'I'm sorry, I didn't mean to be rude.'

We sat and watched the yachts on the water and for some time neither of us spoke.

'I'm falling in love with you already, Ilse,' he said suddenly, putting his hand over mine.

I shrugged. 'Sorry, Frank, I haven't forgotten John yet. I probably never will. I loved him too much.'

He took his hand away and, leaning back in his chair, fished a packet of cigarettes out of his trousers pocket.

'How old are you?' he asked.

'Twenty.'

'Do you suggest that at twenty you've made up your mind to be a widow for ever and just live for a dream of the past?'

I stared at him in surprise. The idea had never occurred to me, but suddenly I realized my position. Was I really prepared to give up the natural life of a normal woman, or did I still want a husband and children, even if I could not have John?'

I looked up at Frank and drew a deep breath. 'No,' I said. 'I don't think I could do that. It would be too hard.'

Frank put his hand back over mine and smiled. 'Thank God for that,' he said with a deep sigh. 'Everything's all right then.'

I didn't see Frank again before he left two days later, but we had parted with the promise to write to each other regularly.

When the time came for me to return I did not want to go. I had grown very fond of John's parents, and I was certain that they were fond of me. Apart from that, the newly found luxury and wealth by which I was surrounded did not leave me unimpressed, and the love and attention lavished upon me by my parents-in-law were something I did not want to lose. When I finally left Mother's parting words at the train were: 'Come back soon, darling, we need you so. Your parents have still got your sister, whereas we have no one.'

From the open window of the train I looked down into her face, and my heart ached. How humble, helpless and bereaved she looked, and how very much like John! I was determined then to return as soon as possible.

Two weeks later the final confirmation of John's death came through. German troops had taken the area and found the remains of the aircraft, and the Russians claimed to have buried the charred bodies of the pilot and his gunner. This was the final destruction of any small hope we might have had, and I felt that I should be with my parents-in-law now. I handed in my notice at the aerodrome, which was accepted at once. I had been with the air force for almost two years, and as six months was the actual time required for any voluntary service I was free. For the moment the Government had no claim on me. My parents were heartbroken and I hated myself for hurting them, but my mind was made up. I felt that John's parents needed me more than ever before, and I needed them.

Before I could start my medical training I had to do three months' practical nursing. It was one of the many new regulations brought out by the N.S. Government. My parents had secured a vacancy for me in one of the hospitals in my home town, so I returned there, having received instructions from the N.S. students' association to report for duty at six-thirty on the morning of 15th October.

It was still dark when I wheeled my bicycle out of the shed, and a cold wind swept through the streets as I pedalled the four miles to the hospital, which was situated on the outskirts of the town. Scrubbing floors and washing dirty bed-pans would be my lot, as of all student nurses before me, and that thought shocked me. But I need not have worried. The hospitals were far too short-staffed now to afford to have young nurses in the sluice-room all day. I was put on proper nursing straight away. It was hard work and the hours were long, from six-thirty in the morning until nine and sometimes ten o'clock at night. The only free day was Sunday.

I stood it for a little while, but at the end of the second week I fell terribly ill. I had contracted one of the worst types of jaundice. When, a fortnight later, I woke from my stupor, for I had been given morphine at intervals, I found my father-in-law sitting at my bedside.

'Hallo, Sparrow,' he said, 'how are you now?'

'How long have I been like this?' I asked, trying hard to keep my eyes focused. 'I'm dreadfully tired.'

'So you are,' said Father, nodding his head in agreement. 'You've been ill for over a fortnight. What do you expect?' He got up and stroked my hair gently. 'When you are well you are going to come back with me. Mother and I will do all we can to get you on your feet. We'll go and rob the farming relatives of all the little nest-eggs they've hidden away in their larders, and then we'll feed you until you are fit and strong again.'

Acknowledging the seriousness of my recent illness, the students' association gave special permission for me to postpone my practical nursing until after the first semester at the university. They did, however, insist that I should take my training at Leipzig, as I had enlisted there the previous year.

I went back to Westphalia with my father-in-law just before Christmas, thus making sure that my parents-in-law would not be on their own during this lovely, nostalgic, Christian holiday. Mother met us at the station, and we walked back to the house in an unhappy silence.

Christmas Eve came. It was for my sake that they had bought a Christmas-tree, and for my sake that the candles were lit and the old carols sung. At eight o'clock that night they took me to hear the traditional singing of 'Silent Night, Holy Night' from the tower of the old Petri Church. I had never seen or heard anything like it before. Tears were streaming down my face as I stood there in the large square in front of the church looking up at those young boys and girls on the balustrade of the church tower, waving their lanterns and singing the beautiful old Christmas carols.

'Gloria, Gloria, in excelsis Deo.'

That night we sat and talked for hours. Father and Mother told me little anecdotes from John's childhood. Sometimes we even laughed. They were tireless in their efforts to make me forget my misery, while their own hearts were aching with the knowledge of their loss. Bit by bit I began to relax.

The licence for the marriage came through early in 1943. According to regulations the ceremony had to take place in the register office of my home town, and we went along to the big grey stone building opposite my old school. My parents and my parents-in-law were with me. The registrar showed us into the room which was usually reserved for weddings. A radiant young couple had just come out and the room was still decorated with spring flowers. A large polished oak table stood in the centre, with the register and some ink-pots and pens on it. The registrar asked me to sit down at the centre of the table opposite him. A chair was then placed on my left with an air force cap and sword on it. My father took a chair at the left end of the table and John's father one at the right.

'You realize, of course,' began the registrar, 'that this is a ceremony which cannot be conducted in the usual manner. These marriages after death are sad affairs, and before we start I should like to express my deepest sympathy with you all for the loss you have suffered.'

I glanced across at John's father and saw him squirm with embarrassment. The registrar then shook hands with each of us in turn, and the ceremony began.

'Miss Ilse H.,' he said, 'a special licence for a marriage after death to your betrothed, John William P., flight-lieutenant in the German Air Force and son of Charles P., of S. in West-phalia, Germany, born on 25th June 1921 at S. in Westphalia, has been granted to you by the Führer.

'Your betrothed, Flight-Lieutenant John William P., was killed in action at Shebekino in Russia, near Kharkov. You

H

will have to sign the marriage register on his behalf with a large cross.

'I ask you now, Ilse H., spinster and daughter of A. H. of A., born on 25th January 1922, if you are prepared to become the legally wedded wife of John William P. If that is your wish and will, will you please answer me with a clear "Yes."'

'Yes.'

'Thank you. Will you please sign the register here.' He put a pen in my hand and, bending over the big book, pointed at a dotted line. 'And for your husband here, with a cross.' He moved his finger a little to the left.

'And now the two witnesses, please,' he said, looking up at the two fathers.

I signed my name and put the cross. The room was deathly still. The pen scratched and got stuck several times in the hard rough paper. The two fathers signed their names and then we sat down again.

'Ilse P.,' the registrar concluded, 'I declare you now the legally wedded wife of John William P., entitled to call yourself Mrs and to take advantage of all the privileges which are included in the status of a married woman.'

He bent across the table and shook hands with me.

'Congratulations,' he said.

Then he turned to John's father trying to do the same, but my father-in-law turned hastily away, ignoring the gesture. We all rose to go, but before we left the room the registrar asked us to wait for a moment. We stood there, feeling a little embarrassed, and while we were waiting John's father took a little box from his trousers pocket.

'Here are your rings, darling,' he said to me, 'both of them— one for you and one for John. You will wear them, won't you? Come here, let me put them on your finger.'

I held out my right hand and he slipped them over the third finger. Then he bent my hand into a fist and put his own over it, gripping it so tightly that I thought for a moment he would crush my fingers beneath his. I looked up, stifling a little moan of pain, and our eyes met. For a moment I thought it was John who was looking down at me so lovingly. The moment passed and John's father turned away quickly. There were tears in his eyes.

Presently the registrar came back with a parcel in his hands. It was the size of a book and I looked at it, wondering what it might be that he was going to give me. He put the parcel into my hand and bowed.

'Madam,' he said, 'I have the honour to present you with a gift from the German Government and our Führer in gratitude for the sacrifice you have made by giving your husband for Germany. Our beloved fatherland and the Führer are sincerely grateful.'

I walked out of the register office in a daze. Once outside I started to unwrap the parcel, and the brown packing paper revealed a black leather case with a book inside. I removed the book from the case and to my utter amazement found myself staring at the words, printed in gold lettering: 'Adolf Hitler, *Mein Kampf.*'

7

MEDICAL STUDENT

The doctrine of 'unconditional surrender' was proclaimed by Churchill and Roosevelt, meeting at Casablanca in January 1943. In May 1943 the Axis armies in Africa surrendered; the Möhne Dam was bombed and breached. By the summer of 1943 the battle of the Atlantic had been won by the Anglo-American navies, the Germans were retreating in Russia and Sicily had been invaded. The Italian campaign opened in September, but was soon bogged down for the winter. The first half of 1944 saw Europe waiting for invasion: Anglo-American forces landed in Normandy on 6th June 1944. By mid July the Russian armies had torn open the German front in the East and were pressing forward on to German territory; by the end of July the German armies in Normandy had collapsed. In September British, American and Russian troops had closed the ring round Germany on both sides and were standing on German soil. Allied air attacks, since the bombing of Hamburg in May 1943, had risen to a crescendo; forces of over a thousand bombers were employed on several occasions and these were far more formidable aircraft than the German bombers of 1940; they carried a bomb load enormous in comparison. More important, the German air defences were weakening, and the morale of the population, especially in the bombed areas, was crumbling.

AFTER the wedding I went back to Westphalia with my parents-in-law, and when I said goodbye to my father and mother at the station I was sure that they felt they had lost their younger child for ever.

In April I began my medical training in Leipzig, and soon found myself a pleasant bed-sitting-room in a large block of flats very near the various laboratories and lecture halls. Chemistry, physics, zoology and botany were the order of the day at this stage. There was no practical anatomy as yet and as far as I could see little to do with medicine. I passed successfully a few minor examinations but, to be quite frank, I felt bored and disappointed. I was glad when the semester was finished. After a short stay with my own parents I went back to Westphalia and John's home town, where it had been arranged with the authorities of the local hospital that I should do my practical nursing.

The Möhne Dam was bombed in May 1943, and when I visited my parents-in-law a few days afterwards we went up to have a look at the damage. The whole area had been cordoned off, but it was perfectly possible to see the gap from a distance. It was about three hundred yards wide, and hundreds of men were already working furiously at the restoration of the huge, solid wall. Five months later the gap was closed. An artist who witnessed the bombing from the top of a hill afterwards described it:

> I was hurrying along the hill road when an enemy aircraft came sweeping into the valley. A few moments later there was an explosion, and another and another, and for a few seconds nothing seemed to happen. Suddenly I saw part of the wall collapse, and a gigantic white mountain of foam and water went gushing up into the air and then dropped at the other side of the dam into the valley below. The water was sweeping down the valley now at an incredible speed, burying everything under its powerful onrush. It looked like a cloud in the moonlight, beautiful and terrible.
>
> Cars driving along the road in the valley were overtaken by the flood, and I saw the colour of their headlights turn from yellow to green as the water covered them. I watched them go on for a bit, and they began to move more and more slowly until they finally stopped and their lamps went out. I looked for the buildings by the riverside, but there were none: they had all been swept away. The valley looked desolate, as if it had been gouged by a giant's hand.

I met Frank again that summer. He was waiting for me one evening at the hospital gates. He was very reproachful because

I had left his letters unanswered, but I did not regret it. I did not want to get involved with any man again until the war was over. It was the first time that I had seen Frank in uniform. It suited him admirably. Irma had told me that he was a captain in the infantry, and with his outstanding intelligence his friends thought he would go far in his profession.

'Why didn't you answer my letters?' he asked while we were shaking hands. 'You promised, you know.'

'I'm sorry, Frank, but my training started soon afterwards and I was frightfully busy. Then you see all my boy-friends are dead and John was killed. It might go on like that for ever. I honestly couldn't take any more.'

'You needn't worry about me. I'll be all right—I know I shall.'

I nodded. 'I hope so, Frank, and to make quite sure I should like you to stay away from me. I seem to bring people bad luck.'

'Don't be so silly,' he blurted out. 'Or are you just making excuses because you don't like me?'

I shook my head. 'No excuses.'

'Well, what am I waiting for then?' he said, and swept me into his arms and kissed me.

'Heavens!' I exclaimed when I could get back my breath. 'What would my parents-in-law say?'

'Surely your parents-in-law don't expect you to stay single for the rest of your life?'

I thought it over.

'You know,' I said at last, 'sometimes I think they do, or at least they hope I will for their sake.'

'They haven't a hope in the world. By the way, are you going up to the Möhne on Sunday? I could come, and we could meet there.'

'Sorry, I promised my parents-in-law to go with them to see some relatives in the country. It's all been fixed up. I can't possibly back out now.'

'Oh come, come, you could find an excuse surely. The weather is so lovely. Go and see Irma. She'll help you fix something up, and then you two can come up together and I'll meet you there.'

'All right, I'll try, but don't be too sure about it, Frank. I don't want to hurt them. I've got to break this to them very gently.'

We did meet on Sunday and several more times after that, and instead of making excuses I simply told my parents-in-law the truth.

'But Frank's father is only an engine driver,' exclaimed Mother, 'and the family are firm Catholics. Be careful, Ilse. You don't want to get involved there surely? It won't do, you know. The two beliefs won't mix. Consider carefully before you make any promises.'

'I haven't made any, Mother, and I'm not going to. It's just a nice friendship, that's all. Please don't worry.'

'Well, let's hope he sees it that way,' said Father. 'Personally I don't believe in friendship between a man and a woman, not for long anyway. It isn't possible. It's a bit soon though for all this, Ilse, don't you think? Please remember, child, that you are bearing our name now. It's a very good name, and I want it to remain good.'

I knew they would take it like that and I felt a bit guilty. One couldn't really blame them for their attitude. They had accepted me in their family circle without any reservations, cared for me lovingly, spoiled me and helped me in every way as if I were their own child. And now it seemed as if I had already forgotten that I owed all this to John, their dead son.

While I had been busy doing my practical nursing in Westphalia, Leipzig had been the target of several heavy allied airraids. In a very anxious letter my parents asked me to come home as they would like to talk over with me the possibility of a change in university. I returned as soon as my hospital service was finished, and we decided that I should continue my training at the university at Marburg-Lahn, a charming little town in Hessen, generally referred to as the 'small Heidelberg.'

As it had been my intention to train at Leipzig for at least another year I had left several of my belongings in my old digs and one Monday morning early I went back to fetch them. I was looking out of the window when my train drew into the huge station and I was shocked at what I saw. The gigantic hall was just a mass of tumbled-down girders, grotesquely bent metal structures and splintered glass. In order to get out of the station I had to climb over several great mounds of rubble, some of them at least six feet high.

It was worse outside. I looked round and I could see nothing but ruins. The big square in front of the station, which was usually so busy, was almost deserted. There were hardly any trams or buses running, and as my part of the city had been hit particularly badly I had to walk.

I set out, wondering how long it would take me to get there. The journey used to take forty-five minutes, but now, with all the rubble in the streets and the pavements torn up, it would take considerably longer. I was worried about my landlady, hoping that she had escaped, for we had not heard from her since the air-raids had started.

I went across the Bahnhofsplatz up to the Brühl and turned to the left towards Augustusplatz. I stopped and looked round, searching for the spire of the Thomaskirche which should have been quite near, but I couldn't find it. I walked on, picking my way carefully across splintered glass, torn-up pavement, bricks, rubble and iron girders. Not a building was left intact. Many had disappeared altogether, others were just hollow, the inside gone.

There were hardly any pedestrians now, and I looked round feeling a little uneasy. The whole scene was frightening and unreal. Everything was still. The houses, which looked all right from a distance, were just as hollow and broken as the ones I had just passed.

I stopped and considered the situation. Should I go back? I could always collect my belongings later, when the city had been tidied up a little and trams and buses were running again. But then I thought of my landlady. I had to go and see for myself if the house was still intact and how she was getting on.

It took me two hours to get there, walking through ruins all the time, hardly meeting anyone. The house was in a little side street on the left off the main road. I could not see it from the top of the street as it was the last one on the right at the other end.

It was deathly still, there was not a soul in sight, nothing moved. Once again I felt that all this was not real. From the main road all the houses along my street looked normal, but with each step I took forward I was disappointed. I walked on slowly. The empty door frames and window sockets looked sordid and menacing, as if they were going to spill out something evil at any moment. I suddenly felt frightened of those who had died underneath those ruins.

I stood and looked round me, feeling trapped and hopeless. Some sirens were wailing feebly in the distance. I paid no attention. I came to the bottom of the road and stopped at the place where my landlady's house used to be. It was just a heap of bricks.

At the beginning of April 1944 I went to Marburg. This was my second term and the training was beginning to get really interesting.

One Saturday evening I was sitting in my room studying when I heard the doorbell, and a few minutes later my landlady showed Frank into my room. He stood by the door smiling, and I was so surprised that I just sat on my chair and stared at him.

'Aren't you going to say hallo?' he said.

I swallowed and watched my landlady close the door softly behind him.

'Where on earth have you come from?' I exclaimed. 'I thought you weren't due for leave until Christmas.'

'I say, you don't sound very enthusiastic. I'm sorry I barged in on you like this, but there was no time for a warning. This is extra-special leave. Count the stars on my shoulder straps.'

I moved a bit closer. 'Gracious, Frank, you've been promoted! Congratulations, major.'

He smiled and took my outstretched hand. 'Come here,' he laughed, and pulled me into the circle of his arms. 'You might as well kiss me. I've only got five days' special leave and we had better make the best of it. I haven't even been home yet. I had to come and see you first.'

'Are you going to stay then?'

'Of course.'

'Where?'

'Here of course, with you.'

I stepped back, feeling a little apprehensive. 'Not in this room though, surely? My landlady wouldn't allow it, you know.'

My attitude seemed to amuse him. 'Have no fear, my little angel,' he said. 'Such a thing would never cross my mind. I shall find somewhere to go for the night.'

He removed his cap and took off his tunic and put them with his gloves on the little sofa by the table. Then he sat down himself.

'Come and sit on my knee,' he said. 'You know, your landlady was actually most obliging when I came, very amiable and polite.' He chuckled to himself. 'It's the Knight's Cross. It's happened so often before. It always amuses me. They think you are a hero if you carry some high decoration. Personally I don't even think I deserved it.'

'The high command of the army thought so. They don't usually give those medals for nothing. I think it's only fair that a brave man should get his due.'

'Ah, never mind, don't let's talk about that now. How about some supper? I'm ravenous.' He got up and put one of his two big suitcases on the table.

'I've got some eggs and bread and butter. If that'll do for you I'll get it straight away. It won't take long.'

'Look,' he said, and motioned me to come over to the table. I caught my breath when I looked into his suitcase. It was crammed with butter, eggs, bacon, coffee, tea, cigarettes, sweets and chocolates, and at the bottom I saw a bottle of cognac and a bottle of champagne.

'Looks as if you had looted some government store,' I said.

He laughed and shook his head. 'Oh no, not a government store, it's the army stores; and I haven't looted them—I simply relieved them of some of their surplus stuff.'

'Let's have a drink now,' said Frank when we had finished our meal. He got up and fetched the two bottles from the wash-stand where I had put them before supper.

'Any glasses?' he asked.

I shook my head. 'Unless you want to ask my landlady.'

He grinned. 'I don't think so. What have you got?'

'Only our cups.'

'They'll do. Got a corkscrew?'

I produced it from the table drawer.

'Cheers,' he said, after he had poured a good measure of brandy into each cup. 'This is to us and our children.'

I took a sip. 'Children?' I asked, trying hard not to choke with the strong liquid. 'Why children? I haven't even got a husband. Aren't you rushing things a bit?'

'I beg your pardon, madam,' he said with a little mock bow. 'I forgot to introduce myself. Your future husband, at your service, madam.'

I laughed and shook my head, feeling a little exasperated.

'No, Frank, it won't do.   I'm not going to marry anyone until this wretched war is over.   Please try and understand.   I've made up my mind about that.'

'We're going to get married next time I come on leave, and that's that.   You might as well get used to the idea.   We'll have a lovely wedding, in your church and in mine.   We'll give the good old home town something to talk about.'

He stood up.   'I'm going now.   Be ready for me tomorrow morning.   We'll go somewhere out in the country.'

'Where are you going?   You won't get a room anywhere now.   It must be somewhere round eleven o'clock.'

He looked at his wrist-watch, put on his cap and gloves and turned towards the door.   'It's ten-forty-five.   I shall go to the station.   The air-raid shelters are open all night, and there are plenty of beds in there.   It's only one mark a night.   It's a service run by the Red Cross.'

I followed him to the door and we kissed good night.   The next few days we spent in perfect harmony.   I was looking forward to marrying Frank.   He would make a very good husband and he adored me.

I did not leave Marburg for the summer vacation.   I had contracted diphtheria and was ill for several weeks.   As there was no room for me in a hospital I had to stay at my digs and my mother came to nurse me, but as soon as I was well enough to travel my mother took me home with her and I had my tonsils removed.

I returned to Marburg in September 1944.   Germany was on the verge of collapse, though we did not realize it.   According to the Government we were at long last close to a unique victory.

At the end of that term I was supposed to sit for part of my first examination, the half-way stage of my training.   It was quite important and we were all very keen to take it.   Once we had passed it many different prospects would open up to us professionally, should we not want to go on.   In order to confirm the dates I went to the university one morning to make inquiries.   A large crowd of students was hanging round the notice-board.   This was not unusual, but what struck me as odd was that they seemed angry and excited.   Peter, a student who had done anatomy with me, saw me and came running along.

'Come and read the latest—it's the very limit.'   He pulled me towards the notice-board, pushed me right through the crowd of angry students and pointed at the announcement of a new government order.   It decreed that all students, male and female, of the first, second, third and fourth terms, should interrupt their training at once in order to help their fatherland in this dire hour of need.   Victory was on the doorstep and it was up to us now to bring it in.   All students of the abovementioned terms must report for voluntary service at once. There were two alternatives: work in a munition factory or service with the air-defence units.

I looked at Peter and then at the crowd of furious boys and girls around me.   A group of students was hanging around outside the dean's office.   They started to hammer at his door and call his name.   A few minutes later the old grey-haired gentleman appeared on the threshold.   He stood and surveyed the indignant crowd with an air of calm dignity.   Eventually he raised his hands in a soothing gesture and motioned us to be silent.   When all was quiet he let his arms fall to his sides and, smiling a little, started to speak.

'Students, calm yourselves.   You have read the notices and there is nothing I can do to alter the decision the Government has made.   I assure you that I did everything within my power to obtain special permission for those students who are in their third and fourth terms to stay here until after the exam.   It was refused.   I shall, however, be quite honest in telling you that I think it is a regrettable decision, as for some of you it may mean a half-finished training which is worse than no training

at all.   I wish you all good luck and may God protect you.   I
hope that after the final victory I shall be able to welcome you
all here again.'

We shouted and stamped our appreciation and he lifted his
right hand up in a salute before he turned back into his office.
The crowd of disgruntled students soon dispersed and I went to
the post office to ring my parents.   When the call came through
an hour later they were surprised to hear the bad news and
promised to try to find a job for me in one of the local munition factories.

I went back to my digs, feeling lonely and frustrated, but I
did not want to leave Marburg so I decided to stay on for a few
days.   Three days later Irmgart, one of the girl students of
my term, came rushing to my apartment.

'We've got to pack and get ready at once,' she said breath-
lessly.   'There are no more trains for civilians from tomorrow
midnight.'

'What about our papers from the university?   I'm not going
to leave without them.   It will probably take days before they
are ready.'

'Leave them, Ilse, I tell you.   Give them your address—they
can always send the papers on; the main thing is that we get
away at once.   I don't want to be caught here and posted to
some air-defence unit somewhere in the wild East, do you?'

'Of course not.   What about permits for travel, and tickets?'

'I'll go and get them now.   Give me the money and for
heaven's sake pack.'

'What about you?   You've got to get ready.'

'I've done my packing.   Now, let's see.   Give me a pencil
and a piece of paper.'

She scribbled something in a hurry and held the paper out
to me.   'Here, when you go to the university will you give
them my address too?   It's on that piece of paper.   Tell them
to send my papers as well.   I'm off now.   See you tonight
after tea.'

The journey home turned out to be a nightmare. The train was overcrowded when it arrived, and at each station some more people squeezed in. There were no vacant seats. We put our suitcases down on the floor in the corridor and sat on top of them, but eventually the train filled up so much that we had to pile one on top of the other.

We were standing wedged in tightly amongst crowds of people, mostly soldiers; there were very few civilians. An S.S. officer, looking very spruce in his neat black uniform, was sitting on the floor to our left. He made a little polite conversation, but seemed very tired and presently fell asleep. The stretch of corridor on our right was crammed with ragged-looking, exhausted soldiers who had stacked their heavy luggage almost up to the ceiling. Most of them looked starved and haggard, as if they had had neither food nor sleep for days. Cigarettes seemed plentiful though, for they smoked incessantly. At the end of the corridor to the right was the lavatory. It was overflowing with passengers. Three were sharing the seat, while five others were leaning against the walls of the tiny cubicle. The door stood open, wedged against the wall of the next compartment, and some more people were leaning against it.

Irmgart left me at Altenbeken. She had to be lifted out through the window. A few kilometres outside Altenbeken the train stopped suddenly and we were attacked by low-flying enemy aircraft. I could hear them come down in a slow dive and then their guns opened up. I had experienced a little of this before, but then the trains had not been quite so packed. Usually the guard came round and locked all the doors so that we could not get out. Why he did this I do not know, but it gave me a most unpleasant sensation of being trapped. This time the train was too crowded for any guard to move even an inch.

Everybody ducked as the first bullet struck somewhere near by, but there was no room to dive under the benches.

The aircraft went and came back. There was another salvo and an unpleasant 'ping' as the bullet caught on some metal. Then there were suddenly three aircraft circling and diving. I listened to the bullets whistle round the train and sweat broke out all over me. I was desperately frightened. Fear started to work on my bowels and some soldiers hoisted me up and passed me along the line like a parcel to the lavatory.

I arrived home early the next morning. My parents put me straight to bed, telling me that I looked terribly ill, but after a few days' rest I started to get ready for my new job in the munition factory.

8

'THIS IS THE END'

In the West the Allies had advanced over four hundred miles from their bases; their advance slowed down and, against last-ditch German resistance, stopped. The eastern front too was stabilized for the winter. Germany had a last, albeit slight, breathing space. Hitler scraped together still another army and, just before Christmas 1944, directed it against the western Allies in the Ardennes. There was not enough strength behind it, and the gamble failed. Then, from March 1945 onwards, the British and Americans closed up to the Rhine. While the Russians poured in like a tidal wave from the East, the British and Americans crossed the Rhine, encircled the Ruhr, cut off the German garrison in Holland and drove on across Germany to meet the Russians near Magdeburg. On 4th May the German High Command signed a surrender agreement for north-west Germany to come into force the following day. The war ended for Germany at midnight on 8th May.

M Y PARENTS were very happy to have me back.
'At least you'll be with us now,' said Father, 'when everything falls to pieces.'

'Do you really think it will come to that? What about those new weapons everybody is talking about?'

'Frankly, I don't believe in them, and if they do come they will come too late. You young people are always inclined to be optimistic. It's the privilege of youth. But our generation was in the 1914–18 war; we know the symptoms. There is no hope for Germany now.'

The following week I started work in a former sewing-machine

I

factory which was producing armaments and small spare parts which I could not identify. The whole thing was under strict security check, and I had to sign a statement before witnesses that I would not speak to anyone about anything I saw or heard inside the factory. I was taken to a large hall filled with machines. They were all running and the noise was deafening. The lights were blazing. The place seemed unbearably hot. I was handed over to a man of about sixty who took me across to a long workbench where a row of girls were sitting checking spare parts. The man asked me to sit down on one of the empty chairs. The girls did not pay the slightest attention to me, so I sat there for a long time not daring to speak and doing nothing, as the man had gone away without giving me any instructions.

Suddenly I did speak. It was to the tall and beautiful young woman who sat next to me. I asked her how she liked the work. She stopped and looked at me, and I noticed that her lovely blue eyes had in them an extraordinary expression of mingled sadness, pride and arrogance. For a moment we sat and stared at each other, but she did not speak. I repeated my question. Still there was not a word from her, but she put her index finger on her lips and shook her head.

A little later, to my great relief, the staff manager's secretary came along to tell me that I was to work in one of the offices and not at the machines. She showed me to a large pleasant room where an elderly lady, three young girls and a crippled young man were busy typing and adding up figures on their machines. I was introduced to them and they welcomed me very kindly, assuring me that the work was not difficult and that I should like it. The elderly lady, who was the supervisor, got the office boy to bring another counting machine, and after briefly explaining its mechanism she left me to add up stacks and stacks of bills. At twelve-thirty the siren went for lunch time. I usually went home, as work did not start again until two o'clock.

When later I described to my colleagues my strange experience with the machine girls in the big hall, they told me that all those girls were D.P.s from Poland, strictly forbidden by government order to speak to any Germans.

Letters arrived frequently from Frank and in December he announced that he was coming on leave. At five o'clock on Christmas morning he rang up. He was at the station where he was waiting for me to come down and help with his luggage.

I dressed quickly, wheeled my good old bike out of the shed and set off. There were six inches of snow and it was bitterly cold. Taxis were things of the past. I pedalled along furiously, half blinded by the snow which was still falling.

Frank was standing outside the station building, almost hidden by two enormous suitcases. We strapped the cases on to the bike with some rope which as a last-minute brain-wave I had stuffed into my coat pocket. Frank pushed the bike and I carried his haversack and gas-mask. It took us an hour to get home. Mother had some *ersatzkaffee* ready when we arrived, but Frank produced a cigar box full of coffee-beans from one of his suitcases, and Mother made real coffee, the first cup my parents and I had tasted for many weeks. It was delicious.

While we were still sipping our coffee Frank got busy unpacking his cases. There were unknown quantities of foodstuffs, including a full-sized goose. We were overwhelmed; during the last two months we had almost forgotten such things existed. Our daily ration by now consisted of two slices of dark, doughy bread, four medium-sized potatoes, perhaps a little margarine, sometimes some awful jam, and occasionally a little horse meat. While Mother busied herself putting all this food into the larder, Frank opened the other suitcase.

'Want to see your present, darling?' he asked me.

'Yes, please.'

He lifted a large paper bag out of the suitcase and gave it to me.

'Go on, open it,' he urged.

I held it up for a moment and looked at it. It felt very heavy. I folded the top flap back and took a peep inside. There, to my astonishment and delight, was a beautiful fur coat, complete with cap and muff.

As Frank had only been granted ten days' leave we had given up the idea of getting married before the war was over, particularly as we both wanted a proper pre-war wedding. Instead we arranged a little engagement party on New Year's Eve. Only members of the family were there. The allied armies were closing in from all sides now, and we were not really in a mood for a big celebration. Somehow Frank had managed to get two very nice gold rings. At midnight we put them on and kissed, while the family crowded round us, wishing us a happy new year and a successful future.

The last day of Frank's leave came and in the evening I went into his room, which was next to mine. One of his suitcases was on the bed. It was open and he was busy packing. At the sound of the door opening he turned round and looked at me absent-mindedly.

'Just the girl I want,' he said. 'Come over here.' He put down the pair of army trousers he was holding in his hands and pointed to a pile of garments lying on the table.

'Could you find a home for them here, darling?' he asked. 'I really don't want to take all that lot back with me to the front. It'll all be over soon. There's no point in carrying those around with me.'

'That's all right, Frank. I'll put them away in the loft.'

'Oh, and here, my wrist-watch, my leather coat, my good uniform and the leather gloves. Keep those as well.' He placed all those things in a chair with the wrist-watch on top.

'The wrist-watch is a valuable one,' he said, picking it up absent-mindedly. 'Don't want Ivan to have it. He'll only ruin it.'

'Goodness! Do you really think it will come to that? You sound terribly depressed and pessimistic, Frank. What's the matter?'

'If Hitler doesn't get those new weapons out soon, Ilse, then Germany's had it. It's really only a question now of keeping the Russians out so that the other Allies can come in first. The Red Army are a nasty lot. I shouldn't like them to get as far as this town.'

'Do you really think they will come?'

'I hope not. Anyway, we'll try and stop them. But if they do come, Ilse, you must go, you and your family, all of you. Try to get through to the West. Leave everything. Surely your parents-in-law would have you?'

I nodded. I had heard many stories about the conduct of the Red Army during its advance. They were not very pleasant ones. Frank picked up a bundle of socks and something clattered on to the table.

'Hell,' he said, 'my Knight's Cross! I very nearly forgot it. Keep that too, will you? Perhaps it's just as well to leave it behind.'

I took the cross and put it on the table in my own room. When I came back he had locked both suitcases and put them on the floor by the bed.

'Where are the clothes?' I asked.

'I put them in one of the cases. I'm not going to take that either. Better keep myself as light as possible.'

'Goodness, Frank, you do sound grim.'

'It is grim, sweetheart, and we might just as well face it. I must go to bed now, Ilse. I want to get a good night's rest before I start tomorrow.'

He got up and kissed me on the forehead. I felt hurt and disappointed. I had never seen him like that before, so serious and preoccupied. He turned towards his bed and did not speak to me any more. In his mind he was already far away. I watched him fold back the blankets and felt the tears stinging

my eyes.   I knew at that instant that I should lose him too.   I
turned round and left the room quickly.

It was January 1945 and the ring round Germany was closing.
There were 70 million of us.   The Russians numbered 180
million, the Americans 160 million, the British 80 million
whites and, in their empire, many hundreds of millions of
coloured people.   The bulk of the war effort of these three
great nations was now directed against us day by day.

Our few allies soon melted away.   The Germany Army still
numbered many divisions, but they were formidable only on
paper, for many of them were reduced to a few thousand men.
The last of the best fighting formations had been thrown away
in the Ardennes.   Now the Russians flooded into Germany and
the German skeleton divisions opposing them began to dis-
integrate.   Road, rail and canal communications began to
dissolve into chaos under the bombing.   Petrol shortages
grounded the new jet planes and the tanks came to a halt.

The Volkssturm—Hitler's home guard—consisting of old
men and young boys, proved nearly useless; they died, but
without very much effect.   And, with few German fighters
left, the allied air forces could roam above us as they pleased.
The British came by night, the Americans by day, each with a
thousand heavy bombers, flying high in massed formation.
The sirens wailed day and night.   We slept in our clothes,
prepared to run down into the cellar at a moment's notice.
Our suitcases with a change of clothes inside stood ready for us
to pick up beside our beds.

My brother-in-law had to put on his uniform again, even
though his wounds had barely healed.   The Government
fitted him with a comfortable artificial leg, promoted him and
gave him a full-time job in the local headquarters of the forces
as an administrative officer.   Most of the time he worked in
an office sitting down, and if there were any calls to be made

outside an army car was at his disposal. Even then, my sister told me, he used to come home almost every evening weary with pain, his stump sore and suppurating.

Shortly after Christmas two teenage girls joined our household. Both came from well-to-do families in Berlin; their parents had sent them to us because the constant air-raids on the city interfered too much with their schooling. Ann and Carol were both fourteen, full of fun and nonsense, and at once they started to flirt outrageously with my poor bewildered father. They were really charming company. Their coming saved us from having to take a whole refugee family into our home.

I was still working at the factory, and at week-ends I used to get on my good old bicycle for a ride out into the country to beg food from the farms. I never came back with empty bags. Most of the farmers' sons had been my father's pupils at one time or another, and as a little gesture of gratitude they were always prepared to give me something.

On one of those trips a Russian aircraft spotted me, a big, ancient-looking kite, rather harmless, I thought, until the gunner started to let fly. Immediately I was off my bike and into the ditch at the side of the road. I saw the bullets hit the road dangerously near, raising little puffs of dust. Then it went away. When it did not return I went back to my bike, which I had left lying in the road, mounted and rode on. Ten minutes later the Russian was back, and we played our little scene all over again. Even though I was badly scared now, I was determined not to give in, for if you are really hungry a few machine-gun bullets don't matter all that much. Seven times the wretch got me off the bike. When I got home I was bruised and dusty all over, but in my bag I carried a large loaf of bread and four pounds of grey flour. A royal reward for my efforts!

Towards the end of January I received a long letter from Frank. So far he seemed all right. The letter told me nothing about the actual situation at the front.   It was a well-balanced happy letter, full of love and tenderness, and I wondered if at the moment he was in any danger at all.

One morning in February word got round that people had broken into one of the local army food stores.   The store was part of the barracks and about three-quarters of an hour's cycle ride from our house.   Our need for food was so great that I decided to stay away from the factory for the morning and go down to the barracks to see if I could get a share of the loot. Crowds of people were said to be there already getting out sugar, jam and bread.   I grabbed a large bag, and was just getting on my bike when Ann came running after me offering to help.   I did not want her to get involved in a thing like that and warned her, but she would not listen, and despite my protests we were both on our way five minutes later, pedalling along fast.

The place was almost deserted when we arrived, and we thought that the whole thing had just been a joke.   We put our bicycles some hundred yards away from the building against a wall, and assuming an air of innocent indifference strolled over to the barbed-wire fence which surrounded the building.   It was cut and torn in several places.   The holes were big and we passed through easily, determined to make inquiries before we turned back.   Then we came to another fence, much stronger and higher than the first one, and even though the wire had been cut in various places the holes were not very big and we had difficulty in squeezing through.   Our bags got stuck in the wire, and my skin began to creep with an uneasy sensation of danger as I struggled to get them free.   For a moment I looked back anxiously at our bikes by the wall, praying silently that they would still be there later in case we had to get away from this place in a hurry.

We walked over to the large grey building.   A door was open on the right-hand side and there was a ramp running along the whole stretch of the wall, obviously meant for loading and unloading goods. A civilian was standing on the ramp at the corner by the open door. He was watching us silently. We walked over to him and asked what was going on. To our great relief he was quite friendly and told us that a lot of food had been taken out already and that there was still a lot more inside. The store had been broken open early that morning by the population and the looting had been going on until half an hour ago, when a group of N.S.K.K. men in uniform had come along on their motor-cycles and threatened to use their guns. The N.S.K.K. was a mobile organization of the Party and most of the looters had been intimidated and left. Soon afterwards the N.S.K.K. men had gone, except for one who was still inside surveying the damage.

'Do you think there's a chance?' I asked.

'Don't know, miss. Wait an' see. We're all waitin', ain't we? Maybe the chap'll go away soon.'

'And if he doesn't?'

'We'll go in anyway. We're not afraid of one chap as long as the others stay away.'

'Let's wait a bit then,' I said to Ann, so we walked away from the building and hung around by the inner fence.

True enough, when nothing had happened after about fifteen minutes a little crowd of people started to assemble. There were only a few at first and they stood about timidly, but more and more arrived and very soon the space in front of the open door by the ramp was packed with them. No one spoke a word. Ann and I had joined them. Quite suddenly, as if someone had given an order, the whole crowd started to surge forward, pushing and squeezing through the door into the building, and we were swept down some steps and along a passage. I slipped on some substance that was probably jam, and I should have fallen had the crowd not been so thick around me. It was very dark, but eventually the passage opened out into a large basement room. It was dimly lit by daylight which came in through some windows at ground level. Spilled sugar was crunching under our feet and there were large, sticky puddles of jam all over the floor.

Presently our eyes got used to the semi-darkness and we started to look around. The place was littered with empty buckets. Pounds and pounds of sugar and jam had been spilled on the floor. It was a terrible waste and could only be explained by the hurry in which people must have been to get at the stuff and take it away safely.

A sudden commotion behind us made me look round, and to my dismay I saw the N.S.K.K. man pass us, elbowing his way towards the entrance. If he gets out, I thought, he's bound to fetch his comrades back, and then we shall all be in serious trouble. I was worried about Ann. I should never have brought her. She was my responsibility now and if anything happened to her I should be to blame.

'Come on. Let's get going before he comes back,' I said, and pulled her along with me. 'Over there, some jam first.' We picked up a large bucket and dumped it into my bag. There were rows and rows of buckets, stacked on top of one another, right up to the ceiling. Some had tumbled down in the general medley, and Ann tripped and nearly fell over one.

'Now the sugar, quick!' I said, steadying her. We hurried to the far corner of the room. The sugar sacks had been stacked in the same way as the jam buckets, and to our disgust a lot of them had not been opened the proper way by untying the string at the top but had simply been slashed open with knives, so that the sugar could be more quickly reached.

I told Ann to hold her bag open, and as I had forgotten to bring a ladle I had to transfer the sugar from the sack into the bag with my hands. Our bag was not half full when we heard some people shouting outside, and from the anxious note in their voices we concluded that something bad was happening. Then we heard the roar of aircraft engines.

'Get down,' I said, and pulled Ann down with me. 'Yanks!

They would come now. The ammunition depot is next door. We'll be blown sky-high if they have any bombs.'

'Hadn't we better get out quick?' said Ann.

'Not yet. Let's wait a moment.'

Ann lifted herself up on her elbows. The planes had gone away.

'Goodness, Ilse! I'm scared,' she said.

'I think it's unlikely that they've got any more ammunition in there,' I told her.

Voices drifted into the cellar from outside. They were muffled and indistinct. Somebody was shouting and giving orders.

'The N.S.K.K. have come back,' I whispered. Ann did not answer.

Most of the other people were getting out of the cellar in a hurry. We stayed, feeling that this place at the moment was as safe as any. We finished filling our bag with sugar and then looked round for the bread. The planes returned and once more we found ourselves on the ground rolling in sugar. Near by a woman was shovelling sugar into a rucksack with a coal shovel. She had a child tied to her back by means of a large shawl and worked like one possessed, oblivious of anything going on around her, while the child seemed to be sound asleep.

The aircraft went and we could hear the people who had left the storeroom panic outside. Women were shrieking at the tops of their voices. There was the report of a pistol, and someone shouted: 'They are shooting at us. Our own people are shooting at us.'

'We'll never get out of here alive,' Ann said. I made no answer. Things looked bad.

'The Yanks are our only hope,' I said. 'If they cause enough confusion amongst the N.S.K.K. men we might be able to slip out unnoticed and get away, provided our bikes are still there.'

'Let's get some bread,' she said, cheering up a little. 'There's nothing else we can do at the moment anyway. I'm so hungry I could eat three loaves alone.'

'We've only got room for one, Ann. Don't let's overload in case we have to run.'

She nodded and picked up one large loaf from the pile and put it on top of her bag. It was a little quieter outside now and we decided to have a look. We started walking up the dark passage towards the door, but when I turned round I found that Ann was no longer with me. I hurried back towards the cellar, and half way down the passage saw her running towards me brandishing another loaf of bread.

'Are you mad?' I said, feeling very angry. 'You did give me a fright. I don't know what I thought had happened to you.'

'I'm sorry, Ilse. I had to get another one. What's one loaf for a big family like ours?'

'We can't carry that, Ann. There's no room, honestly. We won't stand a chance of getting away.'

Her face was set. 'If the worst comes to the worst I shall throw it away, but we can try, can't we?'

I turned towards the door. There was no point in arguing.

We looked out carefully. The square in front of the building was almost empty, except for a group of about seven N.S.K.K. men and their motor-bikes. They seemed nervous and upset. One of them suddenly went down on his knees and seemed to put his ear to the ground.

'Look at that,' whispered Ann. 'What on earth is he doing?'

At that moment six of the men got on their bikes and departed in a cloud of dust and smoke.

'There's only one left now,' I said to Ann. 'Shall we risk it?'

We stepped outside and made for the fence. The man's back was towards us, but suddenly he turned and had us in full view. For a moment both of us felt that this was the end of our expedition.

'Come over here a moment,' he called, paying no attention to our stolen goods.

'Is one of you a nurse by any chance?' he asked, as we drew level with him and put our bags down right in front of him.

'I've been a medical student. Why?' I asked. 'Has anyone been hurt?'

'Look over there.' He pointed at a little depression in the ground about four feet from where we were standing.

'Who is she?' I asked, drawing in my breath sharply. 'What happened?'

He shrugged. 'We don't know; just saw the woman there lying in that little hole a few minutes ago. The others have gone for the ambulance. Can you tell if her pulse is still beating?'

'I can try.' I picked up the woman's limp hand and searched for the reassuring beat in her wrist. It was there. I put the hand back.

'She's alive. I can feel the pulse. It's a bit weak though. Did she get hurt anywhere?'

'I don't think so,' the man said. 'We turned her over, but couldn't detect anything. I didn't do it,' he added nervously. 'We fired in the air.'

'Probably just shock,' I said. At that moment the other men came back with an ambulance, and in the general confusion that followed Ann and I slipped quietly away.

A week later I found myself looting a goods train full of sugar and potatoes. Owing to the constant air alarm the train could not move on, and soon half the population of the town was busy relieving it of its cargo. I had brought a large sack with me, and in order to fill it I had to get right on top of a pile of rolling and tumbling potatoes. My sack was nearly full when the train suddenly jerked and started to move. There was a terrific scramble. People flung their sacks and other containers on to the loading ramp and hurled themselves after them. Everybody got off safely, but the containers were mixed up and soon we were all fighting for our property. When I had finally managed to tear my own sack away from the clutches of a big elderly man, who insisted that it was his, I dragged it along through the excited crowd to where I had parked my bicycle.

My triumph, however, was not to last long. As I was plodding along on my bike, sweating and panting, an enemy aircraft came sweeping down out of the blue. There was an open doorway near by, so I slipped inside and hid underneath a stone staircase. My bike I left outside against the wall. The plane swept the street with its bullets, and when eventually I felt it was safe to come out of my hiding-place I found my bicycle still there, but the potatoes had vanished. I sat down on the pavement and cried.

Our town was not an important military target. There were a few factories and the barracks with a small garrison, but the more important targets lay outside. We felt comparatively safe. As the war drew to its end, however, we kept the *Drahtfunk* going all day and all night, as the bombing had become really grim over most of Germany.

To get the *Drahtfunk* we had to have a special gadget fitted to the wireless set. A steady 'ping, ping, ping' would then come over whenever there were enemy aircraft over German territory either attacking or on their way to attack. At regular intervals an announcer would give the exact position, number and type of the aircraft and warn the district or town for which the formations were heading. Any alteration in direction was of course reported immediately and a warning given to the town or district concerned. As soon as the enemy aircraft formations had left Germany the 'ping' was replaced by a monotonous 'tick-tock' like that of a clock.

In this way we were able to get our warning when the bombers were still hundreds of miles away, and we knew that we could expect sirens later. Special maps were issued to each household on which we followed the course and progress of the aircraft formations right to their final point of attack.

The *Drahtfunk* had become so much part of our lives that every time the 'ping' came on my little three-year-old niece would get her coat and handbag and scramble under the table, calling 'Attention, east course, taking east course.' For her it was merely a game whose lethal nature she mercifully did not understand.

We adults talked about 'bomb carpets.' Each major attack at that time meant about five thousand tons of bombs dropped, not on any particular target, but on a city or town; after the carpet had been 'laid' the city had presumably ceased to exist, and any military target within it was automatically destroyed with the rest.

During the last few weeks our house had gradually been filled with people who had been billeted on us by the housing office. There were three blitzed families from the Rhine and two refugee families from the East, making seventeen of us altogether: eight elderly people, three of them men, two young women, four children, two young girls and myself.

With so many people in the house and the constant air alarms we had soon worked out a plan for a proper *Drahtfunk* shift duty. Every adult in turn had to sit up at night and listen to the air reports. The first shift was from 10 p.m. until 2 a.m. and the second from 2 a.m. until 6 a.m. This system gave everybody else in the house a chance to get a little sleep between the five trips to the cellar which on an average we now made every night.

One night I was sitting up with a book on *Drahtfunk* duty. It was nine o'clock and the house was completely silent. Everybody had gone to bed early. I switched off the light and flicked up the black-out blind on one window. The room was stuffy and I needed some fresh air. It was a lovely clear night. I opened the window and breathed in deeply, wondering what would happen. It was 13th February 1945.

The 'tick-tock' stopped and there was a momentary complete silence. I closed the window, pulled down the blind and sat down in the dark by the wireless. 'Ping, ping, ping.' The announcer came in and said that large formations of enemy aircraft had just crossed the frontier and were now flying on a direct easterly course, destination or target not yet known. I put on the light and looked at the map. If they stayed on that course it would take them another hour to get here. No point in waking the others just yet. I sat down in the dark again and must have dozed off, for I was woken suddenly by the urgent voice of the announcer: 'Attention, please. Attention, please. Large formation of enemy aircraft, course east, heading for Leipzig or Dresden. An air-raid on one of those cities is expected.'

I switched on the light. It was half past nine. What did he say? Leipzig or Dresden! They would come straight over our town then. Leipzig was only twenty-five and Dresden fifty-five miles further east in a direct line. I banged at all the doors furiously, waking everyone as fast as I could. It was high time; they should be here any moment. We rushed round the house, turning off lights and opening windows, when the first lot came across. The second wave came at about one o'clock in the morning. For three nights in succession we saw the glow of the burning city on the horizon. Dresden, one of the most beautiful towns in Germany, had been erased and about seventy thousand people had perished.

Some weeks later Father woke us up in a hurry, telling us to get ready as a formation of enemy aircraft was heading straight for our area. The announcer on the *Drahtfunk* had issued warnings to Leipzig, Chemnitz and all the surrounding towns. We rushed into the cellar and found all the other families there already. The Rhineland people, who were Catholics, were all huddled together in one corner praying aloud. We found this rather disconcerting, but as they came from Dortmund, which had had so many raids, we thought we understood their feelings. The planes flew away to the east and all remained quiet for a long time. Father was keeping watch outside. Everybody was dead tired, the children were asleep, even the praying had stopped. One by one we made ready to go back to our beds, certain that there would be no more that night. Frau Kurt put her candle down on the floor in the hall. It was burning because we used it as our emergency light in the cellar. At that moment Father came rushing into the house.

'Get down quickly!' he shouted. 'They're coming back and they have dropped flares all over the town.' The candle was left behind in the hall. Frau Kurt was bundled down the stairs by Father, who banged the cellar door shut. Then we waited.

'Mother of God, pray for us,' the Rhineland family started again. 'Holy Virgin, please protect us.' Then the planes came, flying low. We could hear the noise of the engines clearly. For a while they just seemed to fly backwards and forwards as if they were looking for something. The next moment there was an unpleasant whistle, followed by an explosion. In an instant everybody was flat on the floor. The cellar shook, mortar came trickling down, and all was quiet again. We raised our heads, hoping that it was over. There were a few more explosions in the distance and then the aircraft returned. This time the whole earth seemed to tremble. There were a number of crashes outside. It sounded as if the house were breaking into pieces. We listened and then the planes came back. We put our heads down. Nobody was praying now. The mothers were lying on top of their children, protecting them with their bodies. Some of the suitcases came tumbling down the stairs where we had put them when we prepared to go back up. Finally all the noises died down.

After ten minutes we got up and dusted ourselves down carefully. Frau Kurt announced that she was going to see if the cellar door would open. A few seconds later she was back.

'The house is on fire!' she shouted. 'Where are the buckets?

K

We need some sand quick, or we shall never get out of here alive.'

My father, who was always remarkably quiet at moments of universal panic, went upstairs and returned smiling broadly. He was carrying Frau Kurt's candle.

'This was the fire,' he said, handing it to her. 'You left it in the hall burning. Everything's smashed upstairs. The draught coming in through the frame of the front door blew the candle over and the wax started to burn.'

We stayed in the cellar for another fifteen minutes, just to make sure there were no stragglers. When we came out we found that the windows had been torn out of their sockets and lay smashed in the garden, most of the doors had collapsed, part of the ceiling had come down and our beds were covered with stucco and broken plaster. We were too exhausted to care. We made one round of the attic to make sure that there were no hidden incendiaries and then we fell into our dust-covered beds and slept.

Some weeks later I was at work in the factory when the air-raid warning was given. It was nearly lunch time and I decided to go home. All was quiet outside and I was certain that I could get back to the house, provided the air wardens left me alone, as they would take anyone they happened to see in the street to the nearest public shelter.

I ran all the way home and arrived just in time to dive into the cellar. A little later there were a number of explosions in the distance, and that was all. The air seemed quiet and soon we went back upstairs to have some lunch. Afterwards I lay down on my bed and fell asleep instantly. At three o'clock my mother roused me. The 'all clear' had just been sounded and it was time for me to go back to the factory.

A large crowd of people were assembled at the gates. A high-ranking Party official hung around giving orders to a group of N.S.K.K. men. I went in and walked along to the big yard at the back. There were a lot more people there, mostly

Germany—year zero. This photograph, taken by the author's second husband, a British soldier, shows what every German city without exception looked like after the war; the waste of destruction stretches away to the horizon, the only intact building being a giant air-raid shelter (the cube-shaped structure top right).

workers whom I had seen before in the big machine halls. And then I turned round. The whole building at the right had been gashed open from top to bottom. A direct hit, I was told, from a bomb dropped from a single aircraft. The bomb had smashed through the roof and exploded in the big machine hall on the top floor. The floor had collapsed and the heavy machines had crashed through every floor to the cellar where a lot of people, including nearly all the D.P.s and French prisoners of war, as well as many of the German staff, had gone to shelter. The N.S.K.K., together with a group of German workers, were trying desperately to force an entrance.

I helped to clear away rubble and gave a hand where help was needed. A group of French prisoners who had escaped the disaster were working like madmen in a desperate effort to get their comrades out of this death trap. It was useless. Those who had not already been crushed by the machines would have to die down there. It was impossible to reach them. The Party official came in, and after a thorough inspection he called it off. The N.S.K.K. men went away with him, and we were left standing in the yard looking at the gigantic heap of rubble. Our works manager, a man of about sixty, came over and stood silently with us.

'If I could find a crane I could probably do it,' he said. 'We should have to shift those big boulders first and then raise the machines. A hell of a job, but I reckon it could be done.'

'It would take days,' said a worker who was standing near by. 'By the time we have knocked a hole in that lot they'll all be dead down there.'

The manager nodded and made a helpless gesture with his hand. 'It's no good anyway,' he said. 'I shouldn't even have a vehicle big enough to bring the crane here, let alone the petrol to run it.'

Everyone was silent, and suddenly I found myself thinking of the beautiful Polish girl whom I had seen on my first day in the factory. She was down there somewhere, dead or trapped. I wondered if she had a lover or a husband who was waiting for her to come back and who would probably never know how and where she died.

'Let's pray,' said the works manager suddenly. 'It's the least we can do.'

Obediently like children we put our hands together and bent our heads.

'Our Father, which art in heaven,' began the manager, and in three different languages we spoke after him the words of the Lord's Prayer.

After the bombing the factory was closed down, and for the first time since Hitler had come to power I was free. Germany was in a complete state of chaos now. Nobody cared whether we worked or not. It was a strange feeling. We could hear the fire of the enemy armies clearly in the distance. We knew it was the end. Our only concern was that the Russians should not come and capture our town. We were prepared to put up with the Americans.

Our Kreisleiter had decided that the population of the town should have a treat. He had therefore ordered one of the large army stores to be opened and the contents distributed amongst the people. Everything would be free of charge, but ration cards would have to be brought along for stamping on receipt of the goods. We had no idea what we should get. That did not matter. To those who have nothing, anything is something.

The store was a former primary school. I went early in the morning. The noises of battle all around the town were much more distinct now. I could hear the shells exploding and the frequent stutter of machine-guns. Now and then an enemy aircraft came circling low over us, for reconnaissance it seemed.

As I approached the school I could hear singing. I stopped and listened. It was an old German drinking song. I entered the school yard, and a most amazing spectacle met my eyes. A large crowd of men and women were assembled, and they all seemed dizzily happy. There were Volkssturm in uniform, some soldiers, N.S.K.K. men, women old and young, and lots of old men in civilian clothes. Everybody had linked arms and they were rocking to the tune of the song.

The door to the gymnasium was wide open and in front of it on a rostrum stood a man in Party uniform. As I moved closer I saw to my surprise that he was distributing alcoholic drinks. 'Drink, drink, little brother, drink,' the people were chanting. Well, I was certainly going to have my share of this.

I pushed my way through the crowd, using my elbows, stepping on people's toes. They were all too happy to notice. An old man grabbed me and gave me a smacking kiss on my cheek. People were laughing and embracing one another all round me. Even the Party official on the rostrum was in a glorious mood.

'Ladies and gentlemen,' he shouted, lifting up a bottle of red wine. 'And now a bottle of Italian wine. Italy, you understand, the Axis, our gallant allies, Mussolini, fat stomach —too much macaroni.'

The mob roared and started to sing a rather nasty little song about the Duce. The bottle was handed over to the customer nearest the rostrum and immediately replaced by another.

'Haven't you got anything yet?' asked a woman standing next to me in the queue.

I laughed. 'Not yet, but I shall have in a minute. Have you got yours?'

She nodded. 'I'm queueing up for someone else now. How many ration cards have you got?' I showed them to her and she counted them.

'That's enough for at least two bottles, I think,' she said. She pushed me forward and stood on her toes, scrutinizing anxiously the people who were in front of us.

'Don't you think it's a disgrace how drunk some of them are?' she asked.

I smiled. 'Don't be too hard on them. It's almost certainly their last fling; and yours and mine for that matter.'

She stood and thought for a while. 'That's treason, you know, what you've said just now,' she remarked very quietly. 'Don't you believe in those marvellous new weapons the Führer has promised us?'

'I—well, I——'

'Next, please!' shouted the man on the rostrum. It was my turn and I was grateful for the interruption. I got a bottle of brandy and a bottle of champagne.

With a bottle under each arm I proceeded to squeeze my way out of the mob. Many people had uncorked their bottles and were gurgling the liquid down happily there and then. Very few could still walk in a straight line. 'Today we're happy, tomorrow we're dead!' they shouted.

9

UNCONDITIONAL SURRENDER

HITLER'S LAST order was that every town must fight to the last man. Our turn was coming and hasty preparations were in progress. The Kreisleiter called out the whole population to help change the town into a fortress. We dug trenches until our hands were blistered and built rather makeshift tank traps. *Panzerfaueste* (tank-killers) were distributed amongst the members of the Volkssturm. Young schoolboys were told to defend every inch of German soil with their Hitler Youth sheath-knives should the need arise. Bridges were blown up in order to stop the advance of the enemy. Young girls were put behind anti-aircraft guns for which there was no more ammunition. Sixty thousand people were getting ready for the end.

It was May. The air was warm and spring was on the way. Outside the town, quite near now, the guns were booming. We very rarely saw my brother-in-law; he spent most of his time at garrison headquarters, hardly ever coming home even for meals. Quite unexpectedly one afternoon he called to tell us quickly that he wanted us to go into the cellar that same evening at nine o'clock sharp and not move until we heard the 'all clear' sounded. Before we could ask any questions he had left the house, jumped into the car and was on his way back to headquarters.

'Something's going to happen,' said Father as we went back into the house, 'and Heinz knows of course. His work brings him in close contact with the Kreisleiter and the Bürgermeister.'

'It's up to those two now, isn't it?' I asked.

Father nodded. 'I'm afraid so, and let's hope they will make the right decision.'

'Is there any decision to be made? Surely Hitler did that for them in his last order, and I don't believe for one moment that they would dare disobey.'

'They will if they have any sense. The Bürgermeister is all right, but I'm not so sure about the Kreisleiter.'

'But then you forget that the Bürgermeister is only a figurehead. The real boss is the Kreisleiter.'

'That may be so, my dear, but the Bürgermeister is a very sensible man, a former member of the Conservative Party. Under the circumstances I think he would speak up. After all, this town has suffered very little damage, and who would have it destroyed now deliberately!'

'Well, I hope the dear old Kreisleiter will see it that way. You know, I think that despite his age he is an idealist. He has known Hitler personally. He adores him and believes in him. I don't think he'll listen to the Bürgermeister or anyone else for that matter.'

Father thought that over for a while. 'And yet,' he said at last, 'the Kreisleiter is a good old man. It might be possible to make him see reason. I'm not giving up hope yet. Unconditional surrender is the only thing for our little town. We certainly can't save Germany from disaster now.'

'Well, we'll see. Let's do as Heinz told us. Whatever happens the cellar will be the safest place for all of us until the worst is over.'

At six o'clock that evening all the firing ceased and we found the sudden quietness more frightening than the constant noise. At nine o'clock my father shut the cellar door behind the last inhabitant of the house. Everybody settled down in gloomy silence for the last tedious wait. The night wore on and nothing moved outside. We shifted and turned on our uncomfortable chairs, and finally we dozed off.

The clatter of soldiers' boots in the house roused us in the early hours of the morning. We heard the cellar door open and sat up. Our liberators seemed to have arrived. A man in uniform came down the stairs and in the dim light of our candle we recognized my brother-in-law.

'It's all over,' he said. 'You can come upstairs.'

We were too relieved to ask any questions. Later, after we had had a little breakfast, Heinz told us what had happened, and as he spoke English and had acted as interpreter his was in the main an eye-witness account.

Early that morning the Americans had sent a messenger to garrison headquarters demanding that the town should be surrendered unconditionally, otherwise the bombardment over it would begin at 9 p.m. that day. The garrison commander contacted the Kreisleiter and asked him and the Bürgermeister to come along to headquarters as the messenger was waiting. The garrison commander was not entitled to decide anything. The power of decision had been passed on to the Party weeks ago, and even though the Party was now dead he would not have dreamed of doing the only sensible thing and handing the town over without the sanction of the Kreisleiter.

The two gentlemen arrived and once more the American gave his message, pointing out that the town was hardly damaged. When he had finished everybody started to talk at once. The Bürgermeister and the garrison commander urged the Kreisleiter to give permission to hand the town over straight away, whereas the Kreisleiter maintained that Hitler's orders should be obeyed to the last. They argued for some time and angry remarks were flying back and forth, when the American interrupted and told them that he had no intention of wasting his time any further and would return to his unit at once. The gentlemen knew the terms, and if by any chance they should come to an agreement before nine o'clock, perhaps one of them would be kind enough to come and let them know. When he had finished he saluted and left the room.

For a little while everybody sat stunned and in silence. The

Kreisleiter was sweating and wiping his forehead continuously. Once more the Bürgermeister and the garrison commander tried to talk the poor man round to their point of view, but he would not budge. Hitler, he said, would never let his people down; he would come at the last moment and save them from disgrace and humiliation.

'In that case, sir,' the garrison commander said very quietly, 'I shall have to take over from you and put you under arrest. I shall order unconditional surrender.'

The Kreisleiter made no fuss. He was old and tired of responsibilities. For a moment he sat and looked at the garrison commander and then he slumped forward on to the table, put his head on his arms and cried bitterly.

On the last drop of petrol my brother-in-law and the Bürgermeister went out to the American lines to give the enemy their answer. When they returned to headquarters an hour later the Kreisleiter had gone, since there was now no reason for the garrison commander to keep him under arrest. A few weeks later he was dead, preferring death to disillusionment and humiliation.

The rest of the night my brother-in-law had spent at headquarters sorting out files and documents and burning those which were not supposed to fall into the enemy's hands. The Kreisleiter and the Bürgermeister had done the same in their offices and when morning came all was ready. The Americans came into the town unobtrusively and in an orderly way. From our house we could see them march down the main road and could hear the rumbling of their tanks in the distance.

The next few days I spent at home on the balcony sun-bathing. Now and then I could hear the radio van go round announcing the new orders issued by the American military government. Curfew was introduced, and everybody found walking in the streets after curfew hours without a special pass was arrested and kept until the next morning.

At the week-end I suddenly started to develop a murderous

toothache. By five o'clock on Saturday afternoon it was so bad that I phoned my dentist, who agreed to see me at once provided I could get a curfew pass.

It was ten minutes past five, ten minutes after curfew had started. All we could do now was to go out into the street and wait for the military police to stop us, explain the position and ask them to give us a pass. Mother came with me. We had not gone far when a jeep drew up beside us and an American soldier asked us for our pass. In our Sunday-best English Mother and I started to explain why we were out of doors without one, but as we were both a little nervous and excited we must have been somewhat incoherent, for the poor man looked from one to the other without grasping what we were trying to say. Finally I pointed to my swollen cheek, opened my mouth wide and showed him the bad tooth. He understood at once.

'You want a pass,' he said, laughing. 'I see. Go to the town hall, room six.' He saluted and the jeep drove off.

We walked along the deserted streets, doubtful now whether we should get our pass, because it was Saturday afternoon, and in spite of what the American had told us to do we thought there would be nobody working in the office. To our surprise we found there three English-speaking Germans and an American sergeant, and within fifteen minutes we had our pass and were on our way again.

Coming back, another American patrol stopped us. The military police sergeant looked at our pass and then he saw my swollen face. Without as much as one word spoken in explanation, he opened the rear door of his jeep and invited me to get in. I was a little surprised but obeyed, leaving the door open for my mother. But before she had even lifted one foot to climb in after me, the sergeant had shut the door and we were off.

I began to feel uneasy. I had read stories about Americans in German magazines. Kidnapping is a favourite pastime out there, I remembered. Then the sergeant interrupted my trend of thought by asking me to direct him to our house. We arrived, I got out, and the jeep drove away the moment my feet touched the ground. I did not even have time to say thank you.

Later on I went to visit my friends, Lilo and her cousin Friedel. I had met them while I was working at the factory. They came from the Rhineland and lived together in a large flat in a house in the market square. I had not seen them since the occupation had started, and they were delighted when I called.

'Come in, old girl,' said Friedel, who had opened the door for me. 'We've got another visitor already.' She showed me into the drawing-room, where I shook hands with Lilo and another girl, whom I was sure I had seen somewhere before.

'I'm Hilde, you saw me at the factory,' she said. 'I was secretary to one of the managers.' I remembered her then and we settled down to a little chat.

'Have you heard from your husband?' I asked Lilo. She shook her head.

'Not a word. Have you heard from Frank?'

'No.'

'Have a cigarette,' said Hilde, holding out a packet. I took one.

'I say,' I said, twiddling it round appreciatively. 'Where did you get those from?'

She laughed and struck a match for me.

'Shall I tell her?' she said, looking at Lilo.

'You should have come earlier, Ilse,' laughed Friedel. 'Hilde was just telling us all about it.'

'Of course you can tell Ilse,' said Lilo. 'She's all right. I vouch for her.'

'Yes, go on, please,' I begged.

'There's nothing much to tell really. You know I live down by the cinema where the American troops assemble to go in for the evening performance?'

'Yes.'

'Well, one evening I went down to the front door and had a closer look at those men. Just for fun, you know. After that one of them started to hang around our door rather a lot. Sometimes he would even signal if he saw me upstairs at the window. One evening I went down to him. He seemed rather nice.'

She fell silent for a moment, and smiled at me shyly.

'Anyway he asked me if I would like some cigarettes and some chocolate. I said I would. "I give them to you for love," he said. I was very hungry, and I hadn't smoked for weeks. So I got the cigarettes and the chocolate. I thought it would be a bargain. After all, what does it matter? Friend or foe, it's nothing to me. I'm all on my own in the world. All my family were killed in Cologne in an air-raid. My life is my own, if you know what I mean.'

We did know, only too well.

'We are quite close now, like friends,' she went on, 'and what's going on in the world doesn't concern us any more.'

No one said a word after she had finished. It was a lovely evening. The sun was going down behind the houses. The window was open and from the market square we could hear a party of American soldiers playing football. We went to the window and watched them. They had marked the field with their steel helmets and were now busily engaged in a carefree game, assisted by a group of young German children who ran after the ball eagerly every time it rolled out of the field.

A few days later Lilo came to our house in a great hurry.

'Come along, Ilse. Hurry,' she said. 'There are about twenty-four American lorries in the market-place, all loaded with German prisoners of war. If you are quick you can catch them and make inquiries about Frank. They are all from the eastern front and the Americans are taking them into the British Zone for demob. Most of them come from the Rhineland and Westphalia.'

They were still there, waiting, when we arrived. The

drivers were Negroes and they were hanging around patiently, waiting for their order to move on. Crowds of Germans were standing round the lorries, which were packed to capacity with disarmed German soldiers in battle dress. Everybody was asking questions about a sweetheart, fiancé, husband or son. The poor soldiers, tired though they were, tried to pay attention to every one of us.

I asked about Frank, but no one had seen or even known of him. I showed them his picture and gave them the number of his unit. I went from one lorry to another, but not one of the soldiers could tell me anything. I gave up then, consoling myself with the thought that I was not the only one. There were many women here who turned away just as disappointed as I was.

'There's one going to the town where your parents-in-law live,' said Lilo. 'Come along! I'll show you. I've just spoken to him. Perhaps you can get a message through.'

He was an officer, very much like Frank in appearance. He readily agreed to take my message, and I hastily scribbled a few words on a piece of paper which he handed me down from the lorry. Someone put a pencil in my hand and someone else an envelope. I put the address of my parents-in-law on the envelope, sealed it and handed it to the young officer. He smiled and saluted.

The next moment a whistle blew, the drivers got in their cabs and the lorries started to move. The soldiers waved and began to sing a well-known farewell song. We waved back. Tears were rolling down everyone's face as the singing was gradually lost in the distance.

We were having tea at Lilo's house one afternoon when the first Russians turned up. There had been a rumour that they would soon take the town over from the Americans, but we had ignored it. It was the banging of car doors that brought us to the window. A number of American jeeps had drawn up in the market-place, and some soldiers had got out and lined up in military fashion. An officer stood waiting by the jeeps, looking rather bored. Then a car came swerving round the corner and stopped right in front of the line of American soldiers. A Russian officer stepped out, the American officer stepped forward, and the two men exchanged the military salute. They talked for a while, pointing in this and that direction while they spoke. There was no interpreter. The Russian seemed to speak English very well. Presently there was another salute, the Russian got into his car, the American into his jeep, and both drove away in different directions.

10

'*IVAN*'

THE RUSSIANS came overnight. They started pouring into the town when darkness fell and were still marching in the following morning. The Americans had left quietly. With the arrival of the Red Army our whole world suddenly changed; the freedom of western civilization left us for ever, and the Iron Curtain came down.

I saw some of the Russian soldiers that morning. They looked dirty, ragged and utterly exhausted and I felt sorry for them. They plodded on, grim and unsmiling. New posters went up, informing the population that the soldiers would be free to roam at their pleasure for three days, when the barracks would be ready to receive them. Sixty thousand people retired to their houses and locked and bolted the doors behind them.

All remained quiet in our road. After all, the Russians had not come to us as fighting troops: the general feeling of fury and hatred had already died down a little. Curfew remained as it was. Only once, late at night, did we hear some soldiers trying to climb over the front gate after they had found it locked. It was a very high gate with spikes on top, and the men were too drunk to manage it. From that night on we organized a proper patrol. One man in the house was always on duty, watching out for approaching Russian soldiers.

The Russians set up their military government and new orders were issued. The first was that all former Party members should report at the commandant's office. Except for my mother our whole family had to go. We had to queue up, there were so many people waiting. Three Russian

officers were seated behind large desks, fully armed, caps
pushed to the backs of their heads, with an interpreter assisting
each one.

'Name, please?' I looked up; it was my turn.

'You should know my name,' I said, smiling in answer to the
interpreter's question. 'How do you come to be here?' The
Russian officer looked at me and then at the girl who acted as
his interpreter. I had recognized her as one of my former
classmates. She looked at me blankly as if she had never seen
me before.

'May I see your Party book, please,' she said coldly, extend-
ing her hand. I gave it to her, still smiling. She had been a
high-ranking Hitler Youth leader when I had last seen her a
few years ago. She bent over my Party book and scribbled
some notes on a pad which was lying beside the officer on the
desk. Stung by her indifference, I decided to tackle her again.

'Where did you learn your Russian?' I asked. 'They didn't
teach it at our school.' She blushed and looked up. There
was cold fury in her eyes. I grinned. She bit her lip and
looked at the Russian. He was busy twiddling his pencil and
seemed to be paying no attention.

'At a school in Czechoslovakia,' she hissed, hoping that the
Russian wouldn't hear. He did though and she jumped a little
when he rapped the desk angrily with his pencil. He spoke to
her rapidly in Russian. She blushed again, nodded and started
to explain something in that language. The Russian seemed
satisfied, my papers were handed back to me and I passed on
to the next desk.

She was waiting for me outside by the door when I had
finished.

'You bitch,' she hissed. 'If you as much as breathe one
word to anyone, I'll have it back on you.'

'I wouldn't dream of such a thing, my dear,' I said, looking
her up and down. 'You have certainly done well for yourself.
Heil Hitler!'

L

She looked round her in agony, frightened that somebody might have overheard our conversation.

'The safest place is always in the lion's tent. That's what the proverb says,' I added, but she was already hurrying away from me back to her place behind the desk beside her new master.

When the town had surrendered my brother-in-law, owing to his severe war injuries, had not been taken prisoner of war by the Americans. They had been appalled to see a man in his condition still in uniform and equipped him with fully valid demobilization papers, telling him to go home. Now the Russian military government wanted to see him about an urgent matter. When he left home my sister was firmly convinced that she would never see him again. At the military government headquarters an interpreter showed him into an office where a Russian officer immediately started to shout at him. Completely ignorant of the Russian language, my brother-in-law did not know what all the fuss was about, but concluded from the officer's angry tone that something was amiss. He waited, a little flustered, until the torrent of words had died down to a trickle and then asked the interpreter what he had done that was wrong. At the interruption the Russian officer started again, but eventually he calmed down enough for my brother-in-law to find out through the interpreter why he had been summoned.

It seemed that the Russians intended to make him a prisoner of war. Heinz showed them his demobilization papers, but the officer waved them aside. Heinz had been an officer to the last moment of surrender and demobilization papers issued by the Americans were of no account. He was taken away. After a week they sent him back. His war injury had proved too much of a nuisance. This time his brand-new demobilization papers were made out in Russian, and to our great relief they were valid.

We were really starving now. The Russians lived on our

products and there was hardly anything left for us. Most of the time we were too weak to do anything. Even queueing up for what little food there was to be distributed sometimes proved too much. We lay down on our beds and rested, and occasionally we went out and watched the Russians.

My father was obliged to sell his gold pocket watch in order to buy some extra food on the black market. One morning I went with him to a watchmaker friend in order to get some information about black market deals. The friend had many Russian customers and was bound to know how we could best get rid of the watch and make a good profit.

We had been in his shop for some time discussing the matter when suddenly the door flew open and a Russian marched in. He flung his right arm on to the counter directly under the nose of the watchmaker, pulled back his uniform sleeve and pointed angrily at seven watches strapped neatly side by side on his wrist.

'These watches all *kaput*,' he said, pointing at his arm. 'I bring them for repair two days ago.' He lifted up his other arm and extended two fingers. 'Yes, two days, and you give them back one day and say they good and now they all *kaput* again. You sabotage.'

The watchmaker looked at the man and then at the watches.

'Yes, I remember,' he said very quietly. 'You brought those watches to me for repair two days ago and I returned them last night. They were all right then, and now you say they don't go any more?'

The Russian nodded vigorously.

'Da, da, you say they good and I pay.'

'Yes. Can I see the watches, please?'

The Russian undid the straps and put the watches in front of the watchmaker, who picked them up one by one and started to wind them. He held each watch up to his ear and made sure that it was working. The Russian watched him suspiciously all the time. When the watchmaker had finished he put the watches in front of the Russian on the counter. 'Of course, you see,' he said, 'you have to wind them every evening. If you don't do that they won't go.'

For a brief moment the Russian looked at the watchmaker across the counter. Light was clearly dawning. Without a word he started to strap the watches back on his wrist. A blush was spreading slowly over his face. Suddenly he looked up and flashed a rather sweet and slightly embarrassed smile first at us and then at the watchmaker. We smiled back, and with just the trace of a little military salute he walked out of the shop, closing the door quietly.

The Russians set up their headquarters in one of the best and biggest houses of the town, away from the centre on a little hill. Some weeks later the wives and children came to join their menfolk. A lot of modern houses and flats were requisitioned in which the Russian families were soon happily installed. Domestic labour was in great demand and our dear old home help had to leave us to serve a Russian family.

This was a full-time job and her work was well paid. She got a good lunch every day, but was not allowed to take any of the left-overs home for her family. Frequently the Russians were allotted a whole pig which they slaughtered and prepared at the house themselves. They did this quite well, but even so parts were thrown out which under the circumstances would have made a heavenly meal for any hungry German. When she asked permission to take some of those throw-outs away with her, the mistress of the house refused, and before she left in the evening always searched her bag and coat pockets to make sure she had taken nothing.

We had several Russian families living in our road. They were very quiet, reserved and well behaved. We used to watch the children in the morning when they were taken to school. One family had two children, a boy and a girl. The father was a major. The little girl was gay and happy, and her lovely little face was always smiling. The boy was dressed in a uniform that was an exact replica of his father's. He always bore himself gravely and erect.

Every morning, when it was time for school, their father's large limousine drew up outside the house and the chauffeur, a soldier in uniform, got out and ran up the steps to knock at the front door. The children came out. The little boy marched towards the car, very dignified, every inch a future officer of Russia. The chauffeur took his place by the door of the car. The boy stopped and looked at him expectantly, and the man immediately stood at attention. Holding the door open with one hand, he saluted the boy smartly with the other; then the boy returned the salute and got into the car. The little girl followed, dancing along, and as she passed the chauffeur making him a funny face. The man grinned broadly, the girl jumped in, the door was closed behind them and a few seconds later the car drove off. This procedure was repeated every morning, without fail.

In the house opposite lived a young war widow with her two sons. A Russian officer had been billeted on her. He was tall, fair-haired and very good-looking. He never bothered the widow about anything if he could possibly help it, and was so quiet that we hardly knew he was there. His manners were faultless and he never drank. He spoke German and French. We all had a little crush on him, but he tactfully ignored our attentions. He was a kind and generous man, who always gave some of his food ration to the widow and her children, and he never asked for anything in return.

The weeks went by and one day I decided to have a 'hair-do.' When I arrived at my hairdresser's she was so busy that she asked me to come back later in the afternoon. It was long after closing time when I returned, but she was still working and I had to wait a little while before she could come to the counter. The moment she saw me she put her finger on her lips, motioning me to be silent. Then she led me past all the cubicles until we arrived at one of the private rooms at the back of the shop. She closed the door carefully.

'I didn't want to say anything out there,' she said. 'Most of them speak and understand German. It wouldn't be safe.'

Her remark puzzled me.

'Who do?' I asked.

'The Russians of course. They're all having their hair permed.'

'I only wanted to make an appointment. What's wrong with that?'

She laughed.

'You don't understand. It isn't just the women, it's all the men as well. We've been worked off our feet for the last few weeks, and we're booked up for weeks to come. All Russian officers and N.C.O.s, and of course the wives and kids. Everybody. It's something new to them, and it's exciting. Everybody's got to have a go.'

I burst out laughing. 'Not much of a chance for me to squeeze in then, I suppose?'

She shook her head. 'Not really. If you can wait a couple of weeks I'll let you know when things get a bit easier. I'm awfully sorry, but I'm worried about the business, you see. I have to give them priority or they'll close my shop.'

'That's all right,' I assured her. 'I don't mind.'

I was walking towards the door when she stopped me.

'May I ask you a favour?'

I turned round. 'Of course.'

'Would you please not speak to anyone about this, and please don't laugh or even smile when you go back now. They're terribly sensitive about these things, and I would only get into trouble.'

'I won't, I promise you.'

'Thank you very much,' she said, and we shook hands.

From that day on I looked a little closer at all the Russian officers I passed in the streets, and true enough their usually straight, short-cropped hair had in many cases grown longer and very curly. The new hair style was most becoming, I must admit, even though I'm sure it did not comply with army regulations. This was obviously a case of *cultura*, and to have *cultura* was the most worth-while thing in the world to a Russian.

When autumn came the Russians exchanged their summer caps for thick fur ones. The curls became a bit of a nuisance then, for it was extremely difficult to balance the fur caps on top of them, and their owners had to step carefully and delicately, keeping their heads very still as they walked along the pavement.

I once saw a sergeant come riding along the road on a bicycle when a Russian officer stepped out right in front of him and motioned him to stop. The sergeant got off his bicycle, looking very frightened, and the officer grabbed him by the front of his tunic and started to shake him violently, shouting at him all the time in Russian. A little crowd of Germans gathered but the officer paid no attention. He continued to knock the poor sergeant about and finally pulled him away from the bike, grabbed the machine and flung it furiously on to the pavement at the other side of the road. The sergeant stood there, looking shaken and embarrassed. The officer turned to him once more, punched him in the face in a final outburst of anger and sent him sprawling on to the pavement.

One night we had some visitors. It was very late and we were all asleep when they came. A tremendous noise woke us. Somebody was trying to knock our front door to bits. My father got up and dressed quickly. Without putting the light on he opened the window carefully and looked out. It was too dark to see anyone, but from the voices outside he could tell at once that some Russian soldiers were trying to force their way into the house.

Silently, and in complete darkness, Father roused all the women in the house and within seconds we had been bundled out of a basement window. In whispers we were instructed to hide under the bushes and keep absolutely quiet. As soon as we were safely outside Father went to open the front door. Five drunken soldiers came tumbling in.

'We want women,' they growled. 'Have you got any women in the house?'

'We have not,' said Father, eyeing them warily. They were all fully armed and one of them was fingering his rifle already.

'We look, and if you tell lie, you old Nazi swine, we "pang" and you *kaput*, see?' he said.

The others pushed my father out of the way and started to swarm all over the house. They found three sleeping children, some men, but no women. They were furious. Growling and snarling like dogs they left the house, and my father locked the door behind them.

With the arrival of the Americans all the banks had been closed. Now, under the Reparation Scheme, the Russians started to take the money away. Thousands of bundles of bank-notes and papers were flung carelessly on to army lorries, while we looked on in dismay. Then they dismantled the machines in the factories. If a machine was too big they simply knocked a hole in the wall and let it down on ropes. The machines were taken to the station where they stood for months in wind and weather until they were finally taken off to Russia. It was the same with the telephones.

One morning the bell rang, and when I opened the door I found myself face to face with a Russian officer.

'You accordion?' he asked in Russian.

I frowned and looked at him blankly. Realizing that he had not made himself clear, he started to search desperately for the right German words.

'I mean, you play accordion?' he said, demonstrating with his hands the movement of pulling and pushing. I nodded. He was stuck again, and from the expression on his face I could tell that he was turning over in his mind all the German vocabulary he had been taught at school. He opened his mouth, looked at me and shut it again. I was utterly astonished and did not know what to make of all this. He drew in a long breath.

'You sell your accordion?' he managed at last in very halting German.

I shook my head. 'It's not for sale.'

He nodded arrogantly. 'Da, da, it is, I want it.'

I cursed inwardly. No matter what happened, he was not going to have my accordion.

'Who told you I had such an instrument anyway?' I asked.

'Nitchewo' (It doesn't matter), he said, dismissing the question with an impatient gesture of his hand. He started to fumble in his trousers pocket and pulled out some badly creased German bank-notes.

'I give sixty marks, you give accordion,' he said, counting out six ten-mark notes and holding them out to me. I shook my head obstinately. He looked at me for a moment, and all of a sudden he got terribly angry.

'All right,' he said, putting the money back in his pocket. 'I take accordion and you get no money. Come on, show me where it is.'

He stepped inside the hall and looked at me expectantly. I shrugged and went to get the accordion. He was the master, I was the serf. I handed the instrument over silently. For a brief moment he looked me straight in the eyes. An expression of unhappy resignation must have clearly shown in them, for his manner changed and he smiled a little.

'Thank you,' he said, putting the six bank-notes into my hands after all. 'Old woman in your house told.'

'Which woman?'

'Old woman with black hair. You a big Nazi?'

I shook my head and laughed. 'I don't think so, but I know who you mean. She lives upstairs.'

He nodded. 'You must be big Nazi. Woman said so.'

'If I was, then she was an even bigger one,' I remarked tartly.

I don't think he understood, for he turned and left the house carrying with him, of course, my lovely big accordion.

I shut the door and stood there for a moment, looking at the money in my hand.   It was a long time since I had last cried, but now the tears came.   I was not crying for the lost accordion, but for Germany and all the Germans.

As a former member of the N.S.D.A.P. my father was dismissed from his job without a pension.   It was a bitter blow for my parents.   Because of his many years of service my father was entitled to the highest rate of pension in his profession.   All the security for his and my mother's old age was gone, but what hurt him most was the feeling of being disgraced.   The future looked grim.   There was no money coming in now, and what we had saved up and put in the bank had been taken away. Nothing remained for us to do but gradually to sell our valuables, jewellery, silver, expensive china, linen and many other things, and the money we made out of these dreary deals just about kept us alive.

I met my first German deserter at Lilo's house.   He was a young man of twenty named Kurt, and he was now a member of the N.K.V.D., the Russian security service.   He never revealed his family name or anything about his past.   His Russian was fluent, and according to him he acted as a kind of liaison officer between the Russians and the Germans.   He and his girlfriend had come to Lilo's house one day, hoping to hire a room there for the girl.   Someone had told them about the large, almost empty house.   The girl was a refugee from the East, and Lilo had agreed at once to take her in.   They had put up a bed in one of the large bathrooms, as most of the other rooms had been requisitioned for other refugees.   The couple were very grateful, and Kurt made it up to Lilo by bringing in plenty of extra food, most of which he obtained in the black market.

One morning in August I received a note from the labour exchange.   It informed me that under the Reparation Scheme, and as a former member of the N.S.D.A.P., I was required to do some unpaid work for the occupation troops. This work was compulsory and partly punishment. I must report at the labour exchange the following Monday at 7 a.m. sharp. No excuse, except severe illness, would be regarded as sufficient reason for disobeying this order.

As I walked down the stairs on Monday morning at twenty minutes to seven, I ran into Miss Saunders, one of our tenants. The house was quiet; everybody else was still sound asleep.

'Where are you off to so early?' I inquired. She had been dismissed from her job in the post office only a few weeks ago for the same reason as Father. It seemed strange that she should be up so early and on her way out.

'To the labour exchange,' she said, with an embarrassed little smile. 'Got a card a few days ago.'

I caught my breath. 'You too? Can I see it? I'm going there.'

It was the same summons and together we set off, both feeling a little uneasy, wondering just what the day would bring. A large group of women of all ages was waiting there already when we arrived. They were chatting away happily, taking no notice whatever of a nervous little elderly man with thick-lensed glasses who was busy blowing a whistle in an unsuccessful attempt to attract attention. He was cross and excited, and somebody told me that he was appointed to organize us.

'His name's Kaiser, I believe,' said a stout little woman next to me. 'He's half Jew, and they put him in charge of the labour exchange and this mob here.'

Seven army lorries drew up, each one manned by three heavily armed Russian soldiers. Still the women took no notice. There was another sharp blast on the whistle.

'Women,' shouted the little man at the top of his voice, 'women, if you don't stop talking I shall call those Russian soldiers over to help me discipline you.' There was silence for the first time.   The women looked at the little man, whose face was now red with fury.   A rather cynical smile spread over it.

'That's better,' he said.   'Now we can talk.'   He stood for a moment scrutinizing us with satisfaction.   'Line up now, please, and I shall call out your names to make sure everyone is here.   After that you will break up into groups of fourteen and get on those army lorries.   The Russians will take you out to the aerodrome where you will work for them and do whatever job they tell you to do.   There's going to be no shirking, no sneaking around in corners or hiding in lavatories.   You work. You work all day and every day until we feel that you have done enough and paid back your debt to the Allies and people like me for having been a Nazi.   That's all.'

As soon as the name check was over we were pushed up on to the back of the lorries and the Russians drove off with us at breakneck speed.

Everything looked just the same at the aerodrome, except that it was now occupied by the Russian Air Force instead of the German.   We went through the gate and a soldier put up the barrier to let us through.   The lorries took the familiar way up to the exchange, went past it and stopped at some pre-fabricated huts.   A little sergeant and some private soldiers stood by one of the huts watching.   As soon as the lorries had gone the sergeant walked over to us and motioned us to follow him inside.   He spoke a little German.

'Germans *nix cultura*,' he said, with a little contemptuous sweep of his hand.   'Place full of vermin, you clean, we give you bucket and lime.'   And waving us round to the back: 'Come on, I show you.'

He showed us the barrels filled with white powder, also about a dozen fire buckets.   Then he took us into a little kitchen leading off the big hut, pointing out the taps where we could draw the water.   From behind a large boiler he produced six sprays, formerly used for putting out incendiaries.

'Now get on,' he said, gesturing impatiently.   Nobody

moved. We just stood and looked at him and then at the gadgets at our feet, not knowing how to start.

The other soldiers, who had been busying themselves somewhere in the background, drew nearer, watching the scene curiously. The sergeant stood quite still, his quick, intelligent blue eyes moving from one woman's face to the next. He was puzzled, probably wondering if he had a mutiny on his hands. He turned round on his heel, picked up a bucket, filled it in the kitchen, came back and put it with a flourish right in front of the group of silent women. The water slopped over the edge on to the first girl's feet. She jumped back with a funny little squeak, right on to the toes of the girl behind her. There was another squeal and a shuffle, and then everybody burst out laughing; but the one who laughed most was our little sergeant. He was wiping tears from his eyes with a rather dirty handkerchief. When we had all recovered he showed us the amount of lime we had to mix with each bucketful of water; and then we all got busy. The ice had been broken.

Soon the other Russians came to help us to put chairs on the tables so that we should be able to clean the ceiling. There were no ladders, and we now had the extra work of moving the tables, with the chairs on top, around the room. We had also to contend with the lime. Of course it kills bugs and germs immediately, but we were afraid of injury by burns, especially to our eyes. We had to spray the ceiling with our eyes closed firmly, and more than once I nearly fell off my table and chair and might have broken my neck. However, we all managed to get through the day unharmed. At midday we were given some soup and allowed to rest until one o'clock. At six o'clock the lorries called for us and we were taken back to town.

As the days went by the lime started to eat holes into our shoes, and as most of us had only one pair left we took them off. Every day we waded around in about two inches of lime and water and our feet became sore and inflamed.

My feet became so bad that I was taken off spraying and told to do the officers' washing. Together with several other women, I scrubbed away all day at dirty army shirts, pants and vests. Huge tubs with steaming hot soapsuds were placed on the concrete outside the officers' billets and there we stood hour after hour washing and rinsing. After a few days my knuckles were raw and bleeding and I winced with pain every time I had to put my hands back into the hot soapy water.

From time to time little groups of Russian soldiers would sneak up and have a look at us. They would hang around giggling and chatting until a particularly cute one would suddenly slap one of us on the behind. At the sound of the inevitable squeal that followed such a daring action they would always shy away from us like frightened little children, only to return after a few minutes and start all over again. They would try all sorts of little tricks to attract our attention, and were so funny at times that we had to interrupt our washing and laugh with them. In the afternoon some of the soldiers off duty would sit down on the ground near us, their backs against the wall of a building, and sing beautifully.

After a week at the wash-tubs I was put back into the hut, and soon found to my horror that now the Russian officers were beginning to take a fancy to us. Some of the girls rather liked their attentions. They were the ones who, instead of working, were allowed to sit behind the hut in the sun with Russian soldiers, smoking Russian cigarettes. Some of us resisted them.

I had one lucky escape from a Mongolian-looking officer, but fortunately, before he could renew his attempted assault, my feet became so bad that I could no longer walk and I had to see a doctor. The lime had burned deep holes into the skin, the small wounds were running with pus, and I was in considerable pain. My parents called in a skin specialist, who gave me some ointment which he took from his own private store; not the proper stuff, he pointed out, but it should work. Any other kind of medicine or ointment for the purpose was at that time unobtainable. I stayed in bed for a fortnight and very slowly my wounds began to clear up. When my feet had healed reasonably well I started to pack and get ready. I had made up my mind to leave the Russian Zone at the first opportunity.

I realized the difficulties. I should have to cross the border illegally, as no German was allowed to leave the Russian Zone. Thousands of people did it every day nevertheless, though the Russian sentries were ordered to shoot at sight.

As it happened, my girl-friend Lilo and her cousin Friedel were planning the same thing. They had had enough of the Russian Zone and wanted to return to their families in the West.

The husband of one of the young women in our house had come back overnight. He had thrown his uniform away some-where in the East, and marched all the way back. No one had spotted him. He had no demobilization papers and would almost certainly go to a prisoner-of-war camp or a labour camp if the Russians found out that he had deceived them. He and his wife were desperately worried and in a great hurry to return to their home town, Dortmund, with their two young children, before the Russian authorities got wind of the man's illegal freedom.

A young woman with a little daughter suffering from T.B. who lived in Lilo's house also wanted to go. She had had a letter from her husband, saying that he was back in their home town of Dortmund and was waiting for her and the child to join him. He had been taken prisoner by the Americans at the end of the war, and after a few months in a prison camp had been demobilized along with many others and taken back to the West.

There were now five women, one man and three children all wanting to leave the Russian Zone as quickly as possible. We knew one another well, so we decided to go together. We found out that the best place for illegal crossing would be from the south-west into the American Zone. It seemed that there were a lot of adventurous Germans along the frontier who were prepared to guide people across at night for a decent fee. They had lived there all their lives and knew the country so well that they could easily carry on this little underground work without ever being caught.   We could not of course contact any of those men beforehand.   The only way was to do it on the spot.   It was a risk, but we took it without hesitation.

11

JOURNEY THROUGH CHAOS

W<small>E SET</small> off one bright morning in late October 1945. The train was a wreck, its windows broken and its lavatories smashed. It moved almost at walking pace. We did not mind; anything would do as long as we got out of this zone. We were all glad that at last things were beginning to move.

Our first goal was to be Probstzella, a town in Thuringia. It was getting dark when we arrived and we called together a little council of war.

Would it be better to spend the night here or get on a local train and travel down a few miles to the little village at the border where the actual crossing was supposed to take place? If we went on there was a likelihood that we should have to spend the night in the open, which with the children and so many women did not seem safe. But on the other hand we could see how the land lay at the border and possibly even discuss the matter of the crossing with one of those guides without any delay.

'Let's go on,' said Herr Krusta, the young father who had demobilized himself. 'The sooner we're through the better for the children and for us.'

His wife agreed. 'I don't want to stay here,' she said. 'I feel so ill, I want to get home quickly.'

'Angela has a temperature,' said the young woman from Lilo's house. 'I want to get across quickly before she gets worse. She's bound to get better medical attention in the British Zone. Perhaps they can even cure her.'

So on we went and two hours later found ourselves in a

166 TOMORROW THE WORLD

miserable little place at the Thuringian border. We alighted
at the little station and looked round. The moon had come
up and we saw that the village was situated in a valley surrounded by wooded hills. All was quiet; the village had
already gone to sleep. A few street lamps were burning and we
could make out the outline of a row of houses about half a mile
away on the slope of a hill. We decided to inquire there about
beds for the night; but there was nothing.

We went back to the station, much depressed and dis-
heartened, and spent the night on the floor in the waiting-room.
Strange individuals walked in and out all night long and
occasionally a Russian came in and looked round as if he were
searching for someone.

The little girl, Angela, got worse and kept crying and whimpering to herself. At one o'clock in the morning some men
came in and walked over to the bar. They had a long conversation with the proprietor, who apparently stayed up all night
watching the strange medley of people who kept assembling in
the waiting-room. When the men had gone Herr Krusta went
up to the proprietor and asked if he knew anyone who would
guide us across.

'They've just gone,' he said. 'Taking another batch across.
Bit late, aren't you?'

'Were they the ones you've just been talking to?'

The proprietor nodded. He looked up at the clock behind
him on the wall. 'They'll be back by five, I should think.
If you come to the bar then you can talk to them and fix something up.'

The guides returned at a quarter to five. To our dismay
they informed Herr Krusta that they were booked up and could
not guide us across until late that afternoon. We had hoped
that they would take us straight away. However, we agreed at
once, even though they asked for an exorbitant fee. It would
cost us every penny of what we had in our pockets, but if they
got us away the money would be well spent.

As soon as daylight came we left the station and went for a little walk in the village. The countryside was charming. About twenty minutes' walk from the station, on a little hill, we saw the Russian headquarters, a large building with the Soviet flag on top. We walked up to it and had a look. It was swarming with Russians, and to our surprise some of the guides were standing there, smoking and chatting with them. We returned to the station and waited. Punctually at five o'clock the door of the waiting-room opened and a man waved to us to come out.

'Just follow me,' he said, 'and let me do the talking. If the Russians should spot us and say anything don't panic. I know most of them. If they see you're with me they'll let you through.'

We looked at one another. The whole thing seemed too easy to be true; there was bound to be a catch somewhere. The man led us up the road towards the Russian headquarters. We followed meekly, weighed down by heavy luggage and slightly handicapped by the two push-chairs with the younger children in them, Angela and the Krustas' little daughter, a child of two. The little boy was six and strong enough to walk.

It took us forty-five minutes to get up the hill to the front gates of the Russian *kommandantura*, as they used to call their headquarters. A Russian sentry stopped our guide and they started a long conversation, interspersed with much joking and laughing. Our guide offered the Russian a cigarette which was promptly accepted. As far as those two men were concerned we did not seem to exist.

The sun had gone down and it was getting dark very fast. Herr Krusta seemed a bit worried and finally walked over and touched the guide's arm. The man turned round and eyed him angrily.

'Don't you think it's time for us to move on now?' asked Herr Krusta. 'It will be dark in half an hour.'

'Who's guide here, you or me?' snapped the man. 'Why

don't you move on? All you have to do is go down this road as far as the frontier barrier. Nobody will stop you.'

We stared at him in surprise. 'But—but you said you were going to see us through to the other side,' protested Herr Krusta. 'That's what we are paying you for, isn't it?'

The man's eyes were blazing with anger now. 'Look here, mister,' he said. 'I've done my bit. You pay me here and now. This is as far as I'm going to take you and no farther. There is no need.' He pointed down the asphalt road. 'The frontier post is two miles down that road. I have talked to this soldier here and he will let you go. All you have to do now is to get going.'

'But are you sure the Americans will let us come in?'

'Sure. Can I have my money now, please?'

We paid reluctantly. There was something very fishy about all this, and we did not like the idea of walking down that road all on our own in full view of everyone.

We had not gone half a mile when the shooting started. Somewhere up in the woods quite near somebody was having a wonderful time with a rifle. We all felt terribly exposed. Obviously there were Russian soldiers hiding in the woods trying to give us a fright. As one rifle was fired several others answered, and the hills echoed with the sharp whip-like cracks of the explosions. It sounded frightful.

'I'm going back,' said Frau Krusta. 'Please, Karl, let's go at once. They might try to shoot us down. Think of the children.'

Herr Krusta nodded and together they turned the push-chair round. Frau Krusta got hold of the little boy's hand and they walked away.

'Wait for me,' called out the young woman with her little daughter Angela. 'I'm coming with you. Don't leave me here on my own.'

Lilo, Friedel and I saw her catch them up, and then the three of us were alone on this dreadful road with Russians all round us firing their rifles nineteen to the dozen.

'What shall we do?' said Lilo, and sat down on her suitcase. 'The man said it would be all right. I don't really think they are shooting at us. What do you think, Ilse?'

'We could walk on for a bit, but I don't like all this.'

'Weren't we fools to pay the man all that money!' she said. 'I had a feeling that he was up to no good.'

'Don't let's give up just yet,' said Friedel. 'Let's find that frontier barrier and see.'

I looked up at the sky. 'You know, it's nearly dark now,' I said. 'I don't like the idea of skidding about in these woods in the night with Russians all around me.'

Our conversation was interrupted by the frantic tinkling of a bicycle bell. We saw a light behind us in the distance and it grew bigger and bigger very quickly indeed. Then a Russian soldier whizzed past us on a bicycle at breakneck speed. He swerved violently as he drew level with us, and we heard him laugh as we jumped out of his way. We watched him with very mixed feelings as he disappeared into the gloom of the misty evening.

'He didn't stop us though,' said Friedel. 'Shall we go on?'

The shooting had stopped and we reached the barrier without any further interruptions. The Russian soldier was standing there half on and half off his bicycle, talking to an American sergeant at the other side. A number of Germans were hanging around in little groups. They too were obviously people who wanted to cross and were hoping that the American would let them come through.

I walked up to the American sergeant and addressed him across the barrier in English. He seemed a little surprised at first, but when he learned what I had to say he shook his head and answered me with a very bored 'No.'

'He won't let us through,' I said, turning round to Lilo and Friedel, who stood behind me.

Their faces fell. 'Why ever not?' asked Lilo, as if somebody had just refused her a piece of cake. 'What have we done?'

'You know as well as I do that the whole thing is illegal,' I said angrily. 'We've been done by that guide, that's all. All we can do now is go back and try some other way tomorrow.'

She looked fearfully at the dark road behind us. 'I can't go back along that road, honestly, Ilse. Can't you try again?'

'Don't be silly, what's the point? He's only sticking to his regulations. Look at all the others waiting. He's not going to let them through, and he won't make an exception with us.'

'He might. Just try once more, please. You're a good-looker. Take off that fearful scarf and smile. It might work, you never know.'

'I don't think it will,' I said, 'not with that type. He's fat and arrogant, and anyway I hate making a fool of myself.'

'Oh, please, be a good sport and do it. I'd try myself if I could speak the language, but I can't.'

'Oh, all right.' I moved up to the barrier once more and spoke up. The American looked down at me coldly, and the corners of his mouth curled downwards when he saw me take off my scarf and smooth my hair. I was sure he had had that trick played on him before. His brief 'No' made me blush with embarrassment. I felt ashamed and humiliated. Everybody was watching us now, grinning maliciously. I turned away from the barrier and, putting on my scarf, started to walk back the way we had come.

Lilo and Friedel followed me meekly. No one spoke. Darkness received us once more and we plodded on, keeping to the centre of the road in case anyone should jump at us from out of the undergrowth. When we had walked half the distance the shooting started again, and Lilo sat down on her suitcase and declared that she would rather die than walk another step. She was crying, and would not listen to anything Friedel and I said. We pleaded and implored, but she did not move. Finally I decided on action and pulled the suitcase away from under her. She sat down on the road with a bump, howling with rage.

'Shut up!' I said. 'Stop that beastly noise. Everyone within a five-mile radius must have heard that we are here. If we don't get away now anything might happen. Pull yourself together, for goodness' sake!'

I picked up her suitcase and walked off. Friedel kept close to my side and neither of us took any more notice of Lilo. A few seconds later we heard her running after us as if the devil were following on her heels. I carried her suitcase all the way back to the station. We did not speak any more. When we arrived we found all the others in the waiting-room looking very worried.

'You silly girls!' said Herr Krusta angrily. 'I was just on my way out to look for you. Where the devil have you been?'

We told our story.

'You must be stark, staring mad,' he said. 'Anything could have happened to you out there in the dark. My wife was terribly upset when we noticed that you weren't with us any more. I nearly went back then to look for you, but I didn't want to leave the two women with the children.'

'We are very sorry,' I said. 'Anyway we know now that we don't stand a chance of getting through, and the guides are obviously fake.'

'Well, we are all invited for supper tonight,' said Herr Krusta.

'Invited for supper? But who has invited us?'

'That's a long story. My wife and I found a very nice old couple here in the village who will put up for the night the two women with the children. When we came back we walked from house to house and asked for help. At last we found these old people, and they want us all to come tonight and share their meal of hot potatoes and milk.'

'That's very nice of them,' I said. 'Where do they live?'

'Up the hill. Come on, we're late already.'

'It's a blessing really,' said Frau Krusta, taking my arm. 'Our rations are so low; another day and I shall have nothing to eat at all for any of us. I don't mind, but it's the children. They need the food so badly.'

I looked down at her pinched little face, wondering secretly who needed the food more, the mother or the children.

The old couple welcomed us with great kindness. When we had finished our potatoes and milk they even brewed a cup of coffee for us, with a few real coffee-beans in it. A lot of the guides, they told us, were crooks, and it was necessary to know your man before entrusting him with money.

The next morning we went along to fetch the two women and their children and to say goodbye to our benefactors. Back at the station we all turned out our pockets and found that between us we had just enough money for the return fare. We sat there counting pennies and feeling hopelessly depressed. Not one of us wanted to go back.

'Supposing your wife, Herr Krusta, went up to the *kommandantura* with the two children,' I said, 'and begged the commandant to help her?'

Herr Krusta thought for a while.

'What good would that do?' he asked rather hopelessly.

'I don't know really,' I confessed, 'but Russians are very fond of children. I have a feeling that they would help if children are involved, especially if she points out that there is no more food for them.'

'They would send us back to where we came from. That's my guess.'

'They might and they might not. Only a little while ago I heard that in a way they are glad to get rid of some of the hungry mouths in their zone. Food is very short and every person gone is a worry less. It isn't all pure joy for them, I'm sure.'

He smiled then, and turning to his wife, 'How do you feel about it?' he said. 'Would you like to try what Ilse suggests? There's no harm in trying.'

Little Frau Krusta looked at her husband with terror in her

eyes. She shook her head violently. 'No, I would not, Karl. I'm scared to death of them. No, it won't do. We'll have to think of something else. I'm not going.'

'There you are,' said Herr Krusta. 'I knew it and I don't pretend to be sorry that she refused. I don't trust those Russians.'

'I see.' I hesitated for a moment, wondering if I dared put my next proposition to them.

'Would you trust me with the children if I went up? I've worked for the Russians for some time and I know them fairly well. At heart they are not as horrible as everyone says they are. They're just different, that's all.'

'Ann, would you trust her?'

Frau Krusta hesitated for a moment and then she smiled at me. 'Ilse is all right,' she said quietly. 'I'd trust her anywhere. But what if she gets into trouble herself?'

Herr Krusta nodded. 'It's a big risk. Are you sure you'll be all right, Ilse? There's no point in doing anything dangerous.'

I rose. 'I think it will be quite all right. Don't worry. I'll take the children now.'

The commandant was an elderly man with white hair. He listened to my story attentively. He did not speak German very well, and after a few moments motioned me to stop and called in a young Russian soldier to help him. When I had finished the commandant looked me over sharply and then smiled at the children. He turned and said something in Russian to the soldier, who nodded and said 'Da, da.'

'The commandant says that you must bring your party up here, and if you all work for us for several hours then you can go. Our soldiers will show you the way.'

I was overjoyed and rushed back as fast as my feet would carry me.

'I hope it's not another trap,' said Herr Krusta doubtfully when I told them. 'Still, let's do as they say. I shouldn't be at all surprised to find that the Russians treat us better than our own countrymen did.'

It was midday when we arrived at the *kommandantura* and the Russians put us to work at once. We were not the only ones there. A lot of other men and women were already busy sweeping, scrubbing and chopping up wood. At two o'clock a Russian sergeant with a rifle over his shoulder ordered us to assemble in the yard outside the building. When everybody was there he blew a whistle and three more Russians came out, also with rifles. Then we were all marched out of the yard, across the road and up a little wooded path at the other side of the embankment.

After ten minutes the path changed into a tangle of tree roots, undergrowth and bushes. It was steep now and we found it hard going with our heavy luggage. Angela was delirious. She lay, limp and flushed, in her push-chair, mumbling and whimpering to herself. We had to carry the push-chair, with her in it, every time we came to a particularly steep stretch of wood. The Russian soldiers drove us on, and whenever we made the slightest noise they came rushing along, motioning us to keep quiet.

At one point I fell behind. My heart was racing, my lungs unable to take the strain. I sat down under a tree and was violently sick. I had hardly wiped my mouth when a Russian came sprinting down the hill, pulled me to my feet and told me to hurry. When he saw the vomit all round me he picked up my suitcase and carried it. It was a kind action which I shall never forget.

We arrived at the top at half past three. Here the ground levelled out and changed into a proper path again. About three hundred yards on there was a hut under a cluster of pine-trees. It was the last Russian sentry post before the American Zone. Once more we were put to work. I had to fetch water from a well near by, accompanied of course by an armed sentry. Then we cleaned latrines and gathered wood.

The sun was going down when we were ordered to assemble outside the hut. We were told to line up in single file and the Russians started to search our luggage. With most of the travellers they turned everything upside-down. One woman had to undress inside the hut after they had examined her: they had found a collection of jewels inside her brassière, and of course they took them away. One man, who talked incessantly and thought himself terribly smart, was told very curtly to shut up or he would have to go back. My turn came and one of the young Russian soldiers pounced on my mouth-organ the moment he saw it lying peacefully amongst my clothes.

'Can I have that, please?' he asked politely and in perfectly good German.

I nodded, only too glad of the opportunity to do something that might put him in a good temper. His face lit up, he cradled the instrument in his hand lovingly and played a few little scales. Then he put it in his trousers pocket. 'O.K., you can go,' he said, without searching any further. I smiled. The American expression sounded rather sweet on Russian lips. I shut the lid of the suitcase, locked it and swung my rucksack on my back. Then I walked down the stretch of path which the Russian had indicated. I was on my way to freedom. Only another two hundred yards to go. I could not believe my good luck.

Before me the path led downwards at a rather steep angle. I was standing looking at it when suddenly the atmosphere started to hiss with the sound of rifle shots. It came so unexpectedly that I lost my nerve, took one terrified leap into the air, and rolled down the slope head over heels, with my suitcase tumbling after me. I tried to stop the fall by grabbing a tuft of grass on my way down, but the heavy rucksack on my back made me swing round and round until at last I came to a stop at the bottom of the slope at Herr Krusta's feet.

He had crossed before me and was sitting on a milestone resting. When he saw me he stared for a moment, and then he started to shake with uncontrollable laughter. He seemed to have gone to pieces and I had the unpleasant feeling that I was looking up at a lunatic. However, I picked myself up, got hold of my suitcase and departed down the village street to join the others. They were laughing almost as much as Herr Krusta.

I heard Herr Krusta follow me down the road. He was still laughing.

'I didn't mean to be rude,' he said when he caught up with us. 'I think it's reaction after all the anxiety. I can't tell you how glad I am to be here.'

'I suppose I looked very funny anyway,' I answered.

'You certainly did,' shouted everybody at once.

'What next?' asked Herr Krusta, changing the subject.

'Food first, please, Karl.' Frau Krusta was worried. 'I've got to get some milk for the children.'

'So have I,' said Angela's mother. 'I only hope the poor child can take it, with that horrible cough.'

'Right, the three girls and I look after the children.' Herr Krusta took charge of the situation. 'You and Ann go and find some milk. Meet us at the village pub when you are ready. It's just down the road by that lime-tree. You can see it from here.' The two women nodded and picked up their bags from the push-chairs. 'I will talk to the owner of the pub in the meantime,' said Herr Krusta, taking his little son's hand, 'and find out how we can reach the nearest railway line.'

The owner of the pub was a friendly, elderly man who asked us at once if we had had a reasonably safe crossing. We told him the whole story. Then he went off into the kitchen and brought for each of us a plateful of steaming hot soup quite free of charge and coupons.

'What are your plans now?' he asked, sitting down at our table. 'It's after five and the nearest railway station is miles away. How do you think you are going to get away from here tonight?'

'We thought you might be able to tell us,' said Herr Krusta.

'That's why we came in here. Is there a way? Tonight, I mean.'

'I doubt it. It's rather late. Four miles from here there is a road crossing where you can pick up a timber lorry going into Lichtenfels, which is your nearest railway station. They're cutting down trees round here for the Americans, and there are a great many lorries running. The drivers are German and know the ropes. They'll give you a lift. They pick hundreds up here during the week. But I doubt if you'll see any tonight. They've packed up for the day.'

'Are the lorries empty?' asked Friedel.

The proprietor laughed. 'Of course not, lady, they're loaded with tree-trunks up to the sky. You have to climb up and hang on for dear life. Terribly dangerous business.'

'But will it be all right for the children?' asked Herr Krusta, with an anxious look on his face.

'No, it won't, but they're all doing it. You have no idea what people load on to those trunks. The risks they take! The drivers take no responsibility of course. The trunks are trussed up, but if a rope should come undone and the things start rolling you've had it.'

'And there's definitely no other way?'

'None, unless you want to walk and that would probably take you several days.'

'What about the trains? Are there any going to the Rhineland and Westphalia?'

The proprietor raised his hand in mock despair. 'Good God, man, have you come from the moon? There's nothing at all. It's chaos here everywhere. You might be lucky and find an empty goods or coal train which happens to be going in your direction. That's your only chance.'

We looked at one another in dismay. That was indeed bad news.

'We have no money,' said Herr Krusta. 'Will they let us go on these trains?'

The man spat on the floor and chuckled. 'You won't need any money. The stations are in ruins. There's hardly any railroad personnel there and certainly no ticket office or ticket collector. But if you want to try and get anywhere at all tonight, you'd better be on your way. Go up to the crossroads and see if there are any stragglers. You might be lucky. Some of those lorries come through quite late. If you can't get a lift come back here and we'll put you up for the night somehow.'

We thanked our host and made ready to go. The two women had come back in the meantime, each one carrying a pint of milk which some kind farmer had given her for nothing. Our host stepped outside and showed us the road we had to take. The sun was low behind the woods, casting long shadows. Soon the autumn mist would gather over the meadows and another day would be gone, leaving us with nothing but a desperate hope that eventually we might get to safety.

It was almost dark when we arrived at the crossroads, and the whole place was deserted. We waited for fifteen minutes and ate our last scraps of food. Herr Krusta was the first to hear the roar of engines in the distance. He ran out to the middle of the road and we followed. A convoy of four lorries was rushing towards us. We started to wave frantically. When they were near enough for their headlights to pick us out they slowed down a little, made a neat detour to avoid us and roared on down the road towards Lichtenfels. We stepped back, bitterly disappointed.

A few minutes later we saw more lights coming towards us in the distance and this time the two women stepped on to the road with the children and the push-chairs. We fairly blocked the way and the lorries stopped. There were three this time. The drivers did not say much. They poked out a thumb from the windows of their cabs, pointing to the backs of their vehicles, and waited patiently for us to get on.

We put the luggage up first and tied it to the trunks with

some rope. There was practically no room for human cargo, and the mothers and children were a really serious problem. Frau Krusta was in tears.

'It's much too dangerous, Karl,' she cried. 'I'm not getting on there with the children. Let's go back for tonight and try again tomorrow.'

'It'll be exactly the same tomorrow, Ann,' said Herr Krusta. 'We've got to manage somehow, or we shall never get away from here. Remember, we have no more food and no money; this is our only chance.'

'If the women don't mind squeezing in with us,' said one of the drivers, 'they can sit with the children in here.'

With a sigh of relief Frau Krusta climbed up into the cab of the leading lorry and Herr Krusta handed her the children. Angela and her mother went in the second truck.

Soon we were under way. The drivers were certainly making up for the delay, and we clung to the tree-trunks like frightened monkeys, hanging on for dear life. At every bend of the road we had to brace ourselves and hold on twice as hard or the centrifugal force would have thrown us off. My muscles ached, my body got bruised as it was flung around on those rough trunks; sometimes I even thought it would be better to let go and have done with it.

Suddenly we drew up. This was the station at Lichtenfels. We got off the vehicles stiffly, unloaded the luggage and thanked the drivers. Gutted buildings, with a few miserable little lights burning, stood where once the station must have been. A tiny electric train was standing on the line, pulsating and all set to start. We jumped on it, children, push-chairs and everything, without bothering to inquire where it was going. It was crowded with humanity to bursting point, and people started to curse as we shoved and pushed and stepped on their toes. In a few minutes it moved out of the station, and I asked a woman standing next to me where it was bound for.

'It's a shuttle train,' she said, 'running between Lichtenfels and Bamberg, and it's the last one today.   You're lucky.   Are you refugees from the East?'

'From Thuringia.   This is our third day since we left home.'

'Where are you going?'

'Westphalia and Rhineland.'

'My word, you'll be lucky if you ever get there,' she said. 'The whole railway system has broken down here, you know.'

'I know, but we were told that there were some coal trains going that way.'

'Yes, there are, once in a while.   You might catch one at Bamberg tonight with any luck, but be careful.   Bamberg is a dangerous place at the moment.   All those liberated D.P.s are roaming the district and refugees are their favourite victims.'

Black night enveloped us when we got off the train at Bamberg.   We seemed to be the only people there.   There were no lights and the ruins of the station building looked menacing, outlined faintly against the night sky.   The tracks were crumpled up.   We stumbled across them in search of goods trains, but there were none.   A smooth, oily silence surrounded us, only disturbed by sounds belonging to our own imagination or by our footsteps.   Eventually we came to a kind of ramp and climbed on to it.   The children were lifted up in their push-chairs and we settled down close together in a circle, using the suitcases as seats.

'This is an awful place,' said Herr Krusta in a low voice. 'The sooner we get out of here the better.   Ann, give me the big bread-knife from the rucksack.   I want to go exploring and see if I can find anyone who knows what's going on.'

We heard Frau Krusta busy herself with the rucksack and hand the knife over to her husband.

'Thanks, just in case.'   He pushed the knife into the top of one of his jack-boots.   'Now stay here and keep absolutely quiet,' he instructed us.   'I shall not be long.   If you hear anything move, shout as loud as you can.   Friedel, you've got that old walking-stick of yours.   Keep it at the ready.   Any

Just inside the Iron Curtain. On the hill-top (*right*) and just behind the trees (*left*) are two of the machine-gun towers which now watch the frontier. Immediately behind them is the 'death strip,' a ploughed area where any civilian can be shot at sight. The area directly in view is mined and patrolled.

(N.B. This photo was taken in 1958: these defences did not exist in 1945, when the Iron Curtain was leaking like a sieve.)

knives or forks would be very useful in case you're attacked.
Keep your wits about you and don't move whatever you do.'
  We heard him jump off the ramp. 'I'm going now,' he
whispered. We sat in silence listening to the noise of his footsteps as he walked down the track. When it had died away the
black uneasy silence closed around us once more. We waited
a long time. One of the children started to whimper, and we
jumped at the sound.
  'It's Angela,' said the young woman from Lilo's house.
'She's thirsty—the fever's dried her out.'
  'Shhh, not so loud,' whispered Frau Krusta. 'Have you got
anything for her to drink?'
  'No, nothing left.'
  I nudged Frau Krusta and pushed my thermos flask against
her chest. Her hands came up at once and she understood.
  'It's only black coffee, just a drop,' I whispered, 'but I don't
think it will hurt her.'
  We heard the child gulp down the bitter liquid, and to every-
body's great relief she calmed down again. Silence settled
down on us once more.
  'I don't understand where my husband can be,' Frau Krusta
whispered at last. 'He seems to have been gone a long time.
I'm getting a bit worried.'
  I put my arm round her shoulder. 'Don't worry, Ann, he'll
be all right—he's got that knife. Don't forget he's been a
soldier for years.' We lapsed into silence again.
  Suddenly we all saw it, a deep red glow and some smoke some
distance away farther down the track.
  'An engine under steam!' I shouted, forgetting caution.
We were all on our feet now, and the next moment we heard
the clatter of Herr Krusta's boots coming towards us.
  'Quick, get going!' he shouted before he had even reached us.
'There's a goods train going in half an hour. I've spoken to
the driver. We're getting on it. It's going to Würzburg.'
  'Würzburg!' we repeated.
  N

'Bit out of the way, isn't it?' remarked Lilo dryly.

'Oh Lord!' moaned Herr Krusta. 'What does it matter as long as we get out of this hole? I'd rather move sitting on an empty goods train than stay in this death trap.'

The goods train was waiting about two hundred yards farther down the line. We scrambled on it and were dismayed to find that the wagons were flat and absolutely open, with no sides to them at all.

'Let's put the push-chairs in the centre,' said Herr Krusta, 'and we'd best put our heavy luggage round them in a circle to stop them from rolling when the train moves.'

'Shall I take the baby out of the push-chair, Karl?' asked Frau Krusta. 'She's sound asleep.'

'I don't think it's necessary. It seems such a shame to wake her. Leave her. I think it will be quite safe.'

'I shall have to leave Angela in hers, anyway,' said the other young woman. 'She's too sick to be taken out. The push-chair keeps her warm.'

We arranged our luggage round the sleeping children in their prams, and then settled down ourselves.

'This is going to be unpleasant and dangerous, you know,' said Friedel, who was sitting next to me. 'There's absolutely nothing to hold on to. It's all right while the train's stationary, but what's going to happen when it starts moving?'

'We'll all fall off and get killed,' I remarked dryly.

Lilo was lying next to Friedel. 'This is going to be worse than the timber lorries,' she said. 'We've got to do something to make it a bit safer for us.'

We thought for a while, but not one of us seemed to have any bright ideas.

'I'll tell you what,' said Lilo suddenly. 'It's not very cold. Let's take off our coats and button them together.'

'How?'

'What I mean is,' said Lilo, 'let's put the buttons of my coat through the buttonholes of Friedel's, and Friedel's buttons into

Ilse's buttonholes, so that we have three lengths of coat in one stretch.'

'What next?' I asked when we had finished.

'Now we stay just as we are, lying down in a row close together. Put the coat blanket on top of us and tuck it firmly underneath Ilse and me, as we are on the outside. It will keep us warm and at the same time make a neat bundle of the three of us which won't roll off so easily.'

'Ah!' We were overwhelmed.

When everybody was as comfortable as the circumstances would permit, we all settled down in silence once more. Ten minutes went by; twice the engine blew its whistle and the hiss of escaping steam told us that we should soon be on our way. The moon had come up and in the flat grey light we could see now that the train was very long indeed. Suddenly, out of the shadows, we saw some figures moving towards us, slowly at first and then running. There were hundreds of them and they seemed to come from nowhere. When they reached us they jumped on to the wagons and stood there for a moment quite still. Not one of them made the slightest noise, and to us they seemed like an army of ghosts.

Some more arrived and jumped up. Then they all got busy, lifting up heavy suitcases, push-carts and other things. Within a few minutes every single wagon was crawling with grey figures. It looked as if a cloud of locusts had settled on the train. Our own wagon was crowded.

'American patrol is outside the station building,' someone whispered close to my ear. 'If they find us here we'll all have to get off. Where are you going?' I stared at the man in surprise and felt relieved that after all these people were real and quite harmless, out on exactly the same adventure as we were.

'Westphalia,' I said in a hushed voice.

'A long way to go, that,' he remarked, 'but you might be lucky and pick up an empty coal train at Würzburg. I do this sort of thing quite frequently, and I've never been left behind.'

We sat in silence for a moment.

'Listen,' he said suddenly, grabbing my arm. 'They're coming. Oh God, I wish this train would move off before they spot it.'

True enough, I could hear the drawling voices quite clearly. The American patrol were coming. At the moment they seemed to be inside the ruined station building. A little later we saw them on the tracks, coming in our direction. Nobody made a sound, so much was at stake. If they found us they would drive us off the train and take us to the police-station. In the end we should almost certainly be sent back to the Russian Zone.

Suddenly there was a jerk, a shrill whistle, and the train started to move. Everybody relaxed. We stood a good chance now of getting away, even though the Americans were quite capable of stopping the train a little farther down the track; their jeeps were very fast. However, the train soon gathered speed and we left Bamberg and the American patrol safely behind. I stretched out on my back and looked up at the sky. It was a beautiful, peaceful night, but I knew it could be fatal to go to sleep. The jolting and jerking might easily loosen the coat from under me, and I should roll off to my death.

'Karl, the prams!' I heard Frau Krusta scream in a terrified voice. I sat bolt upright, and saw the poor woman clinging with one hand to the handle of a push-chair. 'They're rolling, Karl, for God's sake do something before it's too late.'

In an instant Herr Krusta was on his feet, quite forgetting where he was. He lost his balance and crashed down heavily, knocking over some of the suitcases which we had previously placed so carefully round the prams. The consequences of this impulsive action might have been very serious indeed had not some of the other people acted at once. Some held on to the prams while we put up the suitcases again, and some others steadied Herr Krusta and made him sit down. He was trembling with shock and Frau Krusta was crying. After that the mothers carried their children in their arms for the rest of the journey.

I had stretched out again when another frantic cry made me sit up with a jerk. To my surprise I found that my legs were suspended in space, and I realized with a shock that I had moved right to the edge of the wagon without noticing it. Inch by inch I tried to move backwards, but the train jolted and flung me about so badly that I made very little progress.

'Ilse,' yelled Friedel. 'What are you doing?' Then I felt Friedel's hand in my hair. She was pulling for all she was worth. Somebody else got hold of my arms and tugged, and finally I was back in my old place.

Several times the train slowed down or stopped altogether. Sometimes it stood for more than half an hour. At one point we stopped inside a tunnel and waited for another train to pass us. When it came the noise nearly drove us mad. At last in the grey light of dawn we drew into Würzburg station. We were all exhausted and our bodies were bruised and sore, but we were thankful to have arrived so far on our way.

Würzburg station was a good deal livelier than Bamberg. Our train had even stopped at a proper platform. There were quite a lot of people already there waiting and we started to make inquiries at once. We were in luck. An empty coal train was leaving in about an hour from the same platform, and it was bound for Dortmund.

The train came in. This time its wagons had walls but no roofs, so we all slumped down on the dirty, coal-dust-covered floor and, with our backs against the walls, fell asleep. But now the air turned chilly and damp, and it started to drizzle. Soon we felt too cold to sleep and had to get up frequently and stamp about in order to get the blood circulation going again. Our stomachs were rumbling. We had not eaten since the previous afternoon. Some of the other passengers in our wagon, how-ever, were kind enough to share their meagre ration with us. One of them even offered us a woollen blanket for the sick child,

and her mother wrapped her in it lovingly.   In the other trucks
some people started to sing.   They sang the old German
wander songs which sounded sweet and encouraging to us in
our difficulties.

The whole journey took us three days and two nights.   In
peacetime it would have been a matter of hours.   We stopped
only once, at Hagen, a town on the outskirts of the Ruhr.   We
said goodbye to Lilo and Friedel there, as they were likely to
get a better connection to Duisburg from Hagen than they
would have got from Dortmund.

We reached Dortmund late in the afternoon.   The station
was a shambles of smashed girders and torn-up railway tracks,
and the whole dismal scene was lit inadequately by a few lamps.
It was a misty evening and little clouds of fog were swirling round
the bulbs of the lamps, making everything look even ghostlier.
I parted there from the Krustas and from Angela and her
mother.

As I walked across to the other platform to get my last train,
I turned round once more and waved goodbye.   Herr Krusta
was carrying the little boy and Ann was pushing the push-
chair with the baby in it.   Angela's mother was plodding along
near them.   Their progress seemed painfully slow, for they
were also weighed down by their heavy luggage.   How brave
they were to go on and face whatever lay ahead!

Two years later I went to see the Krustas.   Ann had died the
previous year of consumption, about nine months after the
birth of her third baby, but Herr Krusta and the children were
living in their own house which he had built himself with his
own hands.   I inquired about the sick baby Angela.   They
told me she had fully recovered and was living happily with her
parents and a new brother in a small house not far away.

From Dortmund I caught my train into the heart of Westphalia and my beloved little medieval town near Münster.   It
was half past eight at night when I arrived, and it is impossible
to describe how relieved I felt as I walked along the familiar

streets back to the safety of the lovely big house by the church
and the loving care of my parents-in-law.   John was at my side
during that walk home.   I could feel him near me and wondered
if he had guided and protected me all this way.

My parents-in-law were of course completely unprepared.
There was no post yet between the two zones.   When Father
came to open the door in answer to my urgent knocking he did
not recognize me.   I was ragged and dirty, my face and clothes
covered with grime and coal-dust.   He thought I was a refugee
begging for food.

'We haven't got much ourselves,' he said, before I even had
a chance to open my mouth, 'but I will see if my wife has some
potatoes and a little bread to spare.'

At the sight of Father I suddenly burst into tears.   Then he
recognized me.

'Good God, Sparrow, where do you come from so late at
night?' he cried.   'Stop crying, dear, and come in.'   He shut
the door and locked it.   'Come on now, let's show you to
Mother,' he said, leading me down the passage.   'She'll soon
fix you up.'   And that was exactly what she did.   An hour later,
when I lay drowsy and clean in John's comfortable bed, I
realized once more that even after his death John had made me
one of the most precious gifts on earth.   He had given me his
parents.

12

'TOMMY'

I SLEPT round the clock and woke to a clear bright morning. Mother brought my breakfast up to bed and later on I gave my parents-in-law an account of what had happened since I had last seen them. What really astounded them was that I had arrived without a penny in my pocket.

The lovely old house was the same, but now it was swarming with refugees. Food was terribly short, even though the British Occupation Forces lived on their own rations. The farming members of the family could no longer do much for my parents-in-law, as they were compelled to hand over every bit of food they did not need for their own survival. It was distributed amongst the countless German refugees and the population in the towns.

The British Zone of Germany was an area of about the size of Ireland, and whereas its pre-war population was five and a half million people, it was now housing and feeding eighteen million, even apart from the two million D.P.s who lived mostly in barracks.

Coal had become such a rare commodity that my parents-in-law had disconnected the central heating and put up a little iron stove in one room to serve as living-, dining- and drawing-room for everyone. It was the only warm place in the whole house.

My biggest problem was to obtain permission to stay in the British Zone. Unless this were granted I should not be entitled to any ration cards and sooner or later the authorities would send me back to my home town. The British military government had no wish to add to their responsibilities by taking more and more people in.

188

Luckily Father had some very good connections, and soon he was busy telephoning important people who would be able to help. When he had finished he gave me my instructions. I was to call at various official departments in the order in which he gave them, beginning with the police for registration and ending with the labour exchange for a job. I made this tour without any delay, and when I got back I told my parents-in-law all that had happened, and they agreed with me that obviously the first thing to do was to find work as quickly as possible, as without it I could not in any case stay.

During the next four weeks I lived 'blind' in the British Zone. No permission for me to stay there came through. It was a time of suspense, but I brushed up my shorthand and typing and at last Father had a really bright idea. He knew the German manager of the British P.C.L.U.[1] Father phoned him and found him willing to help. He said he would try to keep the first suitable vacancy for me.

A few days later a card arrived, asking me to call at the P.C.L.U. the following morning at nine o'clock. I was terribly nervous, but the young manager gave me courage. He said that all I needed to do in the interview with the British captain in charge of P.C.L.U. was to say yes and no in the right places. This I felt I could manage.

The captain was a young man with the reputation of being very anti-German. My heart was in my mouth when I settled down in the big chair by his desk and waited for him to speak. Almost immediately I knew why he did not like the Germans. He was a Jew.

He told me rather reproachfully that as a boy of fourteen he had been living with a very nice German family in the Black Forest. They had been wonderful to him and he had loved them as if they had been his own parents. Their sons he had always regarded as his brothers.

[1] Pioneer and Civil Labour Unit, a British Army labour exchange, run by the Pioneer Corps.

'Now suppose,' he said, 'the boys and I had met in this war somewhere out at the front. We should have been trying to kill each other. Brother killing brother. It would have been entirely the Germans' fault for making this war.'

I disagreed. 'For one thing,' I said, 'I never wanted a war, and there are many other Germans who did not want one either.'

'All Germans like war. They love uniforms and military drill.'

'So do the British, do they not?'

'Not to such an extent. Anyway, I think that as a nation the Germans are irresponsible; how could they otherwise have chosen a man like Hitler for their leader?'

'Hitler did very well in the beginning and we believed in him, even though many of us had been very sceptical about him at first.'

'You should have got rid of him later on though, when he started to make trouble.'

'How could we have done? There were some attempts from 1938 on. Stauffenberg was the one who came nearest to it perhaps; but it would have been too late then anyway. You know perfectly well how strong Hitler's hold was on us, physically and emotionally. It all really goes back to the Versailles Treaty and the shame and disgrace the German people felt. Hitler gave them new hope. He restored Germany's honour and pride. It's hard for any great nation, or any nation which considers itself to be great, to be treated as Germany was treated in the Treaty of Versailles. You British should understand our feelings; as far as I can see you are just as proud and arrogant as we are.'

'What about the concentration camps, though, and the Jews? When he started that you should have realized that he was an evil character and got rid of him.'

I shook my head sadly. What could I say to that? It was all quite true—and yet . . .

'First of all, most of us did not know anything about the concentration camps, not at least what was really going on inside them. Those who came back from them were not allowed to talk. As far as the Jews are concerned, I can only say that I knew many people who did not approve, but then, you see, whenever there had been trouble in Germany some Jew or other had been at the bottom of it. Bethmann-Hollweg, the man who signed that shameful Versailles Treaty, was a Jew. We did not know that they did all those horrible things to the prisoners in the camps. All we knew was that they were not very nice places to go to, but we did not think that the prisoners in them came to any harm, until after the war when the Allies found them. Quite apart from that, we adored Hitler too much to believe that he would be capable of ordering anything so mean and horrid to be done to those innocent people.'

'And now you know?'

'I don't know, I really don't. I don't think anybody will ever know the truth about all those things.'

'Tell me, why is it that all of you still come to Hitler's defence whenever the subject is mentioned?'

'I think it's partly psychological. By defending him we are trying to save the last bit of self-respect we've got left. Perhaps subconsciously we feel ashamed of having believed in such a man. We followed him blindly and he disappointed us. It's hard to watch an idol tumble to the ground and smash into a thousand pieces. Don't forget, we loved him, and my personal guess is that he actually hated us. At the end of the war, definitely. He hated his own people for having failed him in bringing all his ambitious dreams into realization. It's a great tragedy, and sometimes I wonder if that was the reason why he drove us so remorselessly right to the last. And we still followed him unquestioningly and gave trust and love in return for hatred. And now, with everything gone, it's just as if someone had told you that your wife, whom you trusted and loved, had been unfaithful to you and betrayed you.'

His face was quite serious, and he was obviously trying hard to put himself in our place.

'And we are the third party,' he said suddenly, 'who have told you about the betrayal, and that's why you don't like us?'

'Yes, I think that's what it is. But what is so hurtful about it is that you didn't just tell us once, you keep on telling, rubbing salt into the wound all the time. Haven't we been humiliated enough? Hasn't Germany been taught her lesson? Can't you let things rest now? We don't ask you to forget. We won't forget either, but sooner or later you'll have to come to terms and try and forgive. You can't blame a whole nation for ever for what their leaders have done.'

He smiled and nodded, and I only hoped that I did not appear to him an unrepentant Nazi.

'There is a vacancy in the military government for an English-speaking clerk,' he said finally. 'I think you will do very well. If you would go there straight away and ask for Sergeant Bond, he will fix everything. Tell him that I'm going to ring him later on.'

He shook hands with me and led me to the door.

'Goodbye and good luck,' he said.

Later on I found that the British were directing their propaganda against the Nazis without its occurring to any of them that their Russian allies also had concentration camps and were responsible for at least as many millions of deaths. Apart from that, they soon forgot Finland. And what about the Poles, whom they had handed over to the mercies of the Russians seemingly without a second thought? If the argument that all Germans were responsible for the acts committed in the name of their Government held good, then the British soldiers I met were responsible for these things. But they did not even seem aware of them.

I got the job in the office of the military government and started work the following morning. The months I spent there were happy, peaceful ones. My English, I admit, was rather poor at the beginning, very stilted and old-fashioned, but it soon improved. All the staff—British and German—were extremely nice and the atmosphere was completely relaxed, without any trace of hatred or contempt.

The officer in charge was an elderly man with whitish hair and a red moustache. He possessed a wonderful sense of humour, and one day when a German girl had called to make a claim because she was pregnant by a British soldier, he confessed to his secretary that he was absolutely at a loss in which file to house the girl's request.

'What do you think?' he said to his secretary. 'Fraternization?' He shook his head. 'No, that wouldn't quite cover it. Anglo-German Relations? No, too generalized. What else have we got?' The secretary put some more files on his desk. He thumbed through them all. 'Now let me see. Ah, here, that's it,' he announced, lifting up a file. 'We'll put it under Entertainment. That's the nearest to it really.'

Later that winter my mother-in-law told me that she had met Frank's mother. They had had an official note saying that Frank was dead. He had been killed in a man-to-man fight somewhere in the East shortly before the war had ended. I said nothing. What was there to say? It was only a confirmation of what I had assumed and guessed for a long time now.

One evening when I came home from work I found an elderly lady waiting for me in the drawing-room. She had come to bring me news from my parents and if possible to take me back for a short stay. She was in great trouble. Her husband had held a high position in the N.S.D.A.P. and so far had managed to escape discovery and arrest. He was hiding in their flat in my home town, waiting for an opportunity to escape to the American Zone. He intended to join their married daughter there, while his wife held the fort in the Russian Zone until they could move their belongings and be reunited at the daughter's home.

It was now officially possible to cross from one zone into another provided there was a good reason. An application had first to be made to the authorities. In the Russian Zone there was always a delay of many weeks before the permission came through, but in the British Zone it was much quicker and the special permits to cross into one of the other zones were quite easily obtainable.

Frau Fall had all those permits and was now travelling regularly from the Russian Zone into the British and American, taking with her every time as many of their belongings as she could carry, and depositing them with her daughter in Stuttgart. On one of her next trips she was hoping to smuggle her husband across with her. His papers would be forged, of course, but she had discovered that she could get them through bribery.

'Why don't you come back with me?' she said. 'Your parents would love to see you again, and it is really quite safe.'

'What about my job?'

'Surely you are entitled to a holiday?' she replied rather casually. 'Ask them to give you a fortnight's leave. We'll be back. It won't cost you your job.'

I got my leave, obtained the official permission from the authorities in the British Zone and packed my bag. A week later we were on our way. The journey was quite uneventful. We had to pass through a camp on the British side and stay there for a few days while we went through the procedure of being deloused, though we were of course completely free of lice. Then the German police on the British side led us across and we were back in the Russian Zone of Germany.

My parents were delighted to see me, but the happiness of our reunion was always slightly dimmed by the anxiety about my safety. Frau Fall had promised to get my documents for the return trip along with her own and bring them to our house; but there was no sign of her. When the fortnight was up I went along to her house and was dismayed to find that she had gone.

It was a terrible shock to all of us. We had not the slightest idea how I could be got out of the Russian Zone now. Frau Fall was the only one who knew all the ropes and had all the

connections. I could not possibly apply for return documents
on the grounds of wanting to go back to my job with the British
military government without immediately arousing suspicion.
My parents made careful inquiries, only to find that we should
never be able to get those documents. Things had changed in
the Russian Zone. The Russians were making it as difficult as
possible now for anyone to get out.

Another fortnight went by and there was still no sign of Frau
Fall. My parents were desperately anxious. Very soon the
authorities would get wind of the whole thing and anything
might happen to me then. Late one evening the doorbell rang
and a few minutes later my father showed Kurt, the young
deserter, into the room. He shook hands with us and sat
down. He seemed ill at ease, and I wondered what he could
have come to see us about. While I was away my mother had
written to me several times telling me that she was engaged in
some black-market business with his girl-friend, but that he
had carefully avoided her and my father since Lilo and I had
left the town. The only time they had spoken to him was when
his girl-friend had pneumonia and Mother had taken her into
our house and nursed her back to health.

'I've come to pay a debt,' he said at last, 'because you were
very good to my girl a little while ago. As you know, I work as
a liaison man for the N.K.V.D. and of course I hear all sorts of
things there.' He sat forward on his chair and looked straight
at me. 'Just a few questions, Ilse. When did you come
here?'

'Four weeks ago.'

'Before that you were in the British Zone for six months?'

'Yes, I'm living there now. I just came to pay my parents
a visit and now I'm stuck here. I want to get back very badly
indeed.'

'Yes, you must, and quickly at that. Someone's been
talking. You are in danger of being arrested as a British spy.'

'A what?'

He nodded. 'A British spy. You've been employed by the British over there, haven't you?'

'Yes.'

'Look, I will tell you what to do. Your mother must go to the town hall tomorrow morning. In the permit office works a very nice girl. I'll give you her name in a minute. I know her very well. Your mother must ask for her and tell her that she comes from me. She knows all about your case, and she'll help you. But please be careful. Make sure no one can overhear the conversation, and none of you must ever breathe a word about this to anyone.'

We promised to be very careful and thanked him for his kindness. He wished me good luck.

Mother went to see the girl and they discussed the matter thoroughly in a quiet corner of the office. Nobody paid any attention to them; there were too many people going in and out, handing in their applications at the various counters. A fortnight later I had my documents. They were forged of course. I was now a refugee from Poland on my way out to the West for repatriation.

My parents came with me to the station. The train was due to leave at ten o'clock in the morning. As we stood there on the platform waiting for it to arrive, who should suddenly turn up but Frau Fall. She smiled most amicably when she saw us, just as if nothing had ever happened. We nodded curtly and paid no more attention to her. A little later a friend of my father's, a former bank manager, came to join us.

'Well,' said my father, 'that's a stroke of luck. Are you going on that refugee train to the British Zone?'

He nodded. 'I'm going to Hanover. I'm taking my little boy with me; my wife and the younger boy are coming to join us later.'

He called out to a boy of about nine who was dawdling around farther down the platform. The little chap came running along obediently, and we shook hands.

The author with her husband and children at their home in England. *Left to right:* Thomas Paul Gray (8), Gabriela Christine (6 months), Alexander Michael (11), Monica Elizabeth (9), and Cornelia Barbara (6).

'I say,' said Father, 'do you think you could keep an eye on our daughter, old man? She's going back to Westphalia. I should feel a lot happier if you did.'

'Of course I will. Come on now. Let's find a compartment and reserve some seats. Then we'll go and put the larger pieces of luggage in the luggage van.'

We travelled all day and arrived at the border station at half past nine at night. It was dark and there were no lights anywhere. It seemed a god-forsaken, lonely place, and there was not even a platform. We jumped on to the tracks and made for the luggage van where we had put our suitcases and rucksacks before we had left my home town. It was a mad scramble. We had to fight for our things. Frau Fall suddenly turned up beside us and asked the bank manager to help her shift her luggage, promising that she would help us with ours afterwards.

Some porters were waiting outside the little station building with their carts, ready to take our luggage to the transit camp near by where we should have to spend the night. Frau Fall got the last porter, put her luggage on his cart and walked off without even bothering to look in our direction. So much for the promise to help!

Half an hour went by before the first porter returned, and when we finally arrived at the camp we were dead tired. We went inside one of the large prefabricated huts, and the first person to greet us there, with a happy, innocent smile, was Frau Fall. We turned away. There were about one hundred beds in that hut. They were stacked in tiers made of wood, and had no mattresses, straw or bedding. We should have to sleep on the bare planks.

Most beds were occupied by no less than three people, and we chose one on the top for the three of us. Father's friend, the bank manager, made a little nest for his son at the foot of the bed. Then he settled me down and finally lay down beside me. We covered ourselves with his blanket, which was big

o

enough to keep all three of us warm.   All night long he kept a
protective arm around me.   In that way we appeared to be a
married couple with one child, and were less likely to attract
the attention of the Russian sentry who patrolled up and down
the gangway.

The next morning everyone assembled on the road outside
the camp.   The porters returned and loaded our luggage on
their carts.   Then off we went to the frontier post, accompanied
by armed Russian soldiers.   There were so many of us that we
covered the best part of a two-mile stretch of road.   The
barrier between East and West was on top of a little hill.   We
were now told by some East German policemen to split up into
three single files, each file walking through between two
Russian soldiers who checked our documents and luggage.
One woman, carrying a large pedal sewing-machine, was
ordered to drop it and leave it by the roadside.   She burst
into tears.

'There goes my bread and butter,' she said.   'I'm a dress-
maker.'

Soon heaps of contraband began to pile up: typewriters,
radiograms, bicycles, pieces of furniture, countless bottles of
schnapps and many personal treasures.   Father's friend and I
got through unchecked, but we had a great moment when we
saw Frau Fall having her luggage thoroughly searched.   She
was still being forced to disgorge as we were passing through,
and we waved as we saw her standing amidst her huge pile of
goods.

'Why me?   Why me?' she was saying to the Russian soldiers.
'Look, they are allowed to get through!'

We walked on for a mile to the British check post, and I felt
so thankful when the first West German policeman came in
sight that I flung my arms round his neck.

He laughed and pointed down the road.   'Run along now,'
he said.   'There's your transport waiting for you!'

I had not lost my job at the military government.   They had kept it for me, hoping that sooner or later I should be able to return. Later that year the Belgians took over the area and the military government was reduced to only a few British officers. Most of us lost our jobs, and I was amongst them.

A few weeks later a new British quartering office moved into the town and a vacancy for an English-speaking clerk was offered to me by P.C.L.U. I started in my new job the following Monday, but a week went by before a tall, bespectacled, indifferent-looking man came into the office and claimed me as his clerk and secretary. We eyed each other with mutual disinterest and a trace of disappointment. I was as desolate and disillusioned as my country, thinking nothing, wishing for nothing and giving nothing. Happiness and unhappiness had met and merged in one straight monotonous line. The only thing I wished to preserve now was my pride, pride before my former enemies.

It took me seven months to realize that I had fallen in love with the man for whom I was now working. I loved poetry, and one day after office hours he told me that he had written some himself. I was at once interested and he asked me if I would type some of his poems for him so that he could compile them in a little book. Later on he came to visit us at the house of my parents-in-law, and we sat by the fireplace and talked for hours. The man I had grown to love and now wished to marry was one of our former enemies, and this for all of us was hard to accept. But common sense helped to bridge the difficulties, and love swept away all doubts.